AGAINST ALL ODDS

Essays on Women, Religion and Development
from India and Pakistan

Edited by

Kamla Bhasin & Ritu Menon (for India)
Nighat Said Khan (for Pakistan)

Against All Odds was first published

by

Kali for Women
B 1/8 Hauz Khas
New Delhi 110 016
India

First published, 1994
Second impression, 1996
Third impression, 1997

Produced and published by Kali for Women in collaboration with Isis
International and the South Asian Women's Forum (SAWF)

ISBN 81-85107-74-2

Laser Typeset by Shruti Designs, New Delhi 110 085
Printed at Pauls Press, E-44/11 Okhla Phase II
New Delhi 110 020

Introductory note

The history of this volume is rather long and chequered. It was in 1986 that we (South Asian Women's Forum, Isis International and Kali for Women) thought of putting together a volume on what we then called "Women, Religion and Alternative Development". In fact what was happening all around us in South Asia almost compelled us to take on the challenge of confronting this hydra-headed phenomenon called "Religion" and to understand how it was affecting women's lives, their status and their prospects for self-realisation and development.

In 1987 in India we witnessed the revival of widow immolation by "modern", "educated" Maruti-driving Rajput men and women. Earlier, in 1985-86, the Shah Bano case led to intense controversies and debates on religion-based personal laws, culminating in the passage of the Muslim Women's (Protection of Rights in Divorce) Bill, which violated all constitutional guarantees regarding equality and fundamental rights. Communal conflicts in cities like Ahmedabad threatened to wipe out the work done by organisations like SEWA, on creating and empowering women's groups across communities and religions.

In Pakistan, progressive family laws were being replaced by Islamic laws which were to drastically reduce women's spaces, choices, status. In May 1991, the Shariat Bill was finally passed by an elected government, subordinating all other laws to Shariat. In Bangladesh, women's organisations and development groups could feel the slow but definite growth of religious revivalism, making it difficult for women activists to work with and in communities. Now, in 1994, there have been cases of fundamentalist Islamic clerics beating a man with shoes and having his head shaved because he taught illiterate Muslim women; and in the first three months of this year religious zealots are reported to have vandalised 1,500 girls' schools and torched 55 of them.

Foiled by these trends many women and men involved with development realised that the whole issue of religion which they had more or less ignored earlier, needed to be addressed, understood and dealt with, especially as it affected their work with poor women in rural and urban areas.

We took on the challenge of putting together this volume because we felt that, in general, many feminists too, have tended to take a categorically anti-

अपने ज़मीर से पूछो आख़िर धर्म क्या है?

religion stand which is not only a-historical, but also unmindful of existing realities. We felt then, and feel so now, that the basic needs of women, as of the poor, have to be seen as linked not only to class and patriarchy as two separate but related categories, but also to religion and community, the third aspect of this trinity.

We have to concede that religion continues to play an extremely important role in determining culture, social interaction and behaviour patterns. The formation of mentalities as an interaction between economic, political, socio-cultural and religious structures thus needs to be understood more clearly. The largely religion-based socialisation of children, for example, determines self-perception and perceptions of the social order, and imposes frameworks on people which they cannot easily break or move away from.

Religion must also be understood because it is often used by the dominant classes in society to maintain their control over people, especially women. The growing trend towards religious revivalism and cultural nationalism on the part of the State and right-wing political parties, and progressive nationalist movements when they assert a national identity by going back to religious roots makes a study of the impact of religion and identity politics on women almost an imperative.

At a meeting in 1987 in Colombo, of women academics and activists from India, Pakistan and Sri Lanka the issue of women, religion and social change came in for considerable discussion. The context was our three countries, seen over the last decade or so, with a focus on the kind of social change taking place in all three, and in which religious and ethnic configurations often formed the critical core. Thus, rather than looking at social change as a pro-gressive, radicalising force, we recognised that the change already under way in much of the subcontinent was retrogressive, often even fascist; that a significant degree of mobilisation had taken place by rekindling fundamental-ist and chauvinist tendencies, and that, in the resulting turmoil, the position of women was under greater threat than ever before, susceptible to the most dangerous notions of what is appropriate and desirable.

The project of Islamisation in Pakistan and Bangladesh and the zealous promotion of a national identity based on it; the crystallising of separatist demands around ethnic or minority claims in all three countries; the visible and vocal presence of fundamentalist conservatism that made itself felt in the Roop Kanwar and Shah Bano controversies in India, and the active propaga-tion by or collusion of the State in all these, have effectively wrenched the issue of religion and identity out of the personal and private domains into the social and public. No matter what our individual allegiances might be in this

Bangla women spew venom at clerics

Farid Hossain

Dhaka

WAVING CARTOONS depicting Islamic priests as demons, about 2,000 women on Wednesday demanded punishment for conservative clergymen campaigning against western relief agencies that are helping women in Bangladesh.

"Down with the preachers" and "Hang the traders of religion to death," the protesters chanted as they marched through downtown Dhaka. Most of them were housewives and members of Women's Development Forum, a new coalition of a dozen women's rights organisations.

It was the first protest against the clerics who want the Government to ban Western aid agencies working to provide jobs, education and health care to women in this impoverished nation of 120 million people, most of them Muslims.

About 800 relief agencies working in the country spend nearly $ 200 million annually on programme for 12.5 million people.

Muslim fundamentalists say the agencies are enemies of Islam because they try to convert poor Muslims to Christianity and encourage the women of this male-dominated society to challenge tradition and come out of their veils.

"The clerics are harassing women," the protesters said in a letter to Premier Khaleda Zia. *AP*

regard, we are now all players in this play of identity politics.

Players we may be, but as women, do we see ourselves as victims, anti-heroines, protagonists or bit-players? Or all of these at some time or another? Moreover, as women involved with other women and with feminism, and with movements for social change, what is our equation with religion? How and what do we believe? How do we reject or reconcile? When the irresistible force of another woman's belief comes up against the immovable object of one's own lack of it, how does one proceed? Are our personal beliefs not a matter of public or, at least, social significance?

At one level, obviously, a woman's concern with what is happening around her is the same as anyone else's and to the extent that religion impinges on all our lives in a palpable way, we must reckon with it. Second, as Fatima Mernissi has observed in the context of Muslim societies, "If we are to assess correctly women's prospects and future . . . we have to relinquish simplistic stereotypes that present fundamentalism as an expression of regressive medieval archaisms and read it, instead, as a political statement."

But, as importantly, we have to move beyond the conventional rejection of religion as "false consciousness", because we are often interacting with women for whom it is an article of faith, in spite of their experience of its oppression. And because we have found that it provides space for manoeuvre, that ironically, it may even "liberate" temporarily—long enough to raise consciousness and mobilise— that sometimes it can be its own worst enemy; and, finally, because we ourselves are often in a predicament regarding our own responses.

Not all of us have been able to categorically reject religion, and even when we do, we have learned to accept its power of persuasion for the majority of women who see it as their salvation, whether or not they are oppressed by it. Then, regardless of belief, have we not all at some time seen the creative and liberating potential of religion and appropriated it for our own purposes? Have we not tried to reinterpret religious texts to our advantage? And are we not perplexed by this ambivalence?

The strategic use of religion by women has undoubtedly been successful in some of our countries, characterised by ideologies of seclusion and exclusion, and by the fact that women, by and large, have faith and cannot be alienated on this score. The question that arises is: how far can religion be used strategically without it, sooner or later, reinforcing those very attitudes and norms that have been oppressive? And is there a qualitative difference between women's "strategic use" of religion and its "misuse" by other groups, including fundamentalist ones? Are they not all operating from within the same parameters?

In the last few years, developments at the national and regional levels have clearly established the political ascendancy of right-wing fundamentalist groups and their ability to mobilise around the issue of minority/majority or ethnic identities. The implication of the State in all these contests for power and contestations over definitions of cultural nationalism and secularism has called for a serious re-examination of the phenomenon of religious revivalism and its political agenda. What has also surfaced during this time is the militancy of right-wing women in all the countries of the region, and their successful incorporation into communal politics. For feminists and for the women's movement this is yet another disturbing dimension of the problem: how, in our work with women, and particularly at moments of acute communal or ethnic polarisation, do we understand women as protagonists of violent and disruptive communitarian politics, most recently witnessed in India with the destruction of the Babri mosque and its aftermath.

At the same time there is the recognition that women's multiple, and often overlapping, identities — of class, community, gender, religion, caste — come into play diversely and at different times; and in direct interaction with wider political, economic and social forces. This factor has necessarily to be accommodated in our analyses, both in theory and on the ground.

The concern with religion, then, expresses itself in several ways: directly, at the level of countering oppression in the name of religion and obstruction in the attempt to realise one's potential, economically, socially and individually; indirectly, at the level of trying to articulate and understand the experience of religion as a humanising force. At another level, it is necessary for us to acknowledge that even within the framework of development, one is often working with women — and men — who are personally grappling with their own response to religion; who are in a genuine predicament when working from within religious or cultural traditions to effect social change, and for whom the adopting of "for or against" positions is a real dilemma, personally as well as in the course of their work. Perhaps most urgently, the concern is with the collusion of right-wing economics and fundamentalist, anti-secular and anti-democratic political practice and its impact on development — and consequently on women.

The essays in this volume address some of these issues in the context of South Asia. We initially identified women activists, academics, journalists and researchers in Bangladesh, India, Nepal, Pakistan and Sri Lanka and invited them to write for us. We suggested that their contributions state or discuss various aspects of the issue and indicate directions for future work in terms of research and action so that we have a better understanding of the linkages between women, development and religion.

In spite of our best efforts we failed to get enough contributions from Bangladesh, Nepal and Sri Lanka, but we did have a sufficient number of thought-provoking articles from Pakistan and India. Since the original idea was to bring out a South Asian volume, we debated whether we should abandon the whole project rather than reduce it to two countries. The final decision, as you can see, was to present what we did have in the hope that this volume will trigger off more sharing and dialogue and, hopefully, lead to more reflection and analysis.

RITU MENON
KAMLA BHASIN
April 1994

Contents

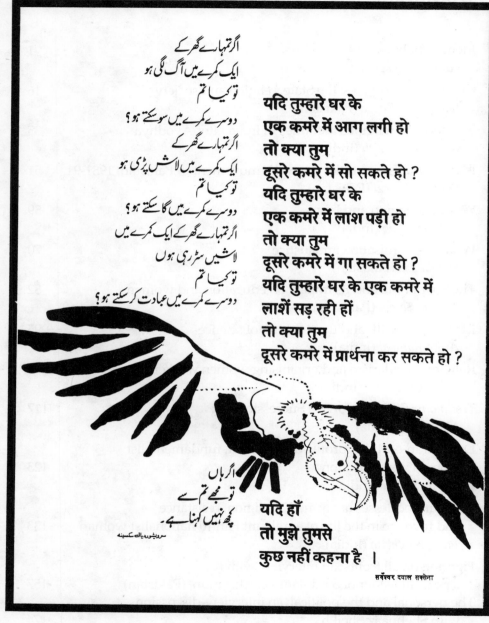

यदि तुम्हारे घर के
एक कमरे में आग लगी हो
तो क्या तुम
दूसरे कमरे में सो सकते हो ?
यदि तुम्हारे घर के
एक कमरे में लाश पड़ी हो
तो क्या तुम
दूसरे कमरे में गा सकते हो ?
यदि तुम्हारे घर के एक कमरे में
लाशें सड़ रही हों
तो क्या तुम
दूसरे कमरे में प्रार्थना कर सकते हो ?

यदि हाँ
तो मुझे तुमसे
कुछ नहीं कहना है ।

सर्वेश्वर दयाल सक्सेना

Design: Zargar Zahoor
Poster: Janatantric aur Dharmnirpeksh Manch, Delhi

Identity politics

Amrita Chhachhi*

In the last decade the S. Asian region has been witnessing a tremendous escalation of communal/ethnic violence, accompanied by the emergence and growth of religious fundamentalism. The general communalisation of society, the erection of barriers of hatred and vengeance between communities, the destruction of life and resources, and the inability of the governments in the region to find a solution reflects a deep-rooted crisis of the nation-state in S.Asia. It is the more depressed sections of society who are most affected by these developments, and we feel that communal/ethnic violence and religious fundamentalism have very specific implications for women. Women are not just victims of violence but are also seen as symbols of communal identities and relations between men and women; the proper role for women in society has become the terrain on which broader issues of differences in economic, political and social power are being fought. This is clear in the process of Islamisation in Pakistan where restrictive laws focus on women, and in the uproar over the Shah Bano case and Roop Kanwar's sati in India during 1985-1987. The issue of identity politics necessarily requires an understanding of women's subordination and highlights the links between other struggles for change and feminism as a political movement.

There were two implicit assumptions in our discussions on identity politics. First, we chose to focus on identity politics rather than communalism and fundamentalism, and this implied a shift in perception, i.e., rather than look at communalism/fundamentalism as forms of false consciousness or merely a result of manipulation by the State and political parties, we were concerned with the question of why people in the S.Asian region responded to and identified themselves with religious/ethnic identities, why this identification aroused such passion and hatred, and why it often overwhelmed either class or regional affiliations in situations of conflict. Is there in fact a national or regional identity in S.Asia today? How far do class and gender form a material basis for identities? Our second assumption followed from the first in looking critically at

*Based on discussions held during a S. Asian Workshop on Women and Development in Bangalore, India in 1989, and taken from the report, *Pressing Against the Boundaries* (FAO- FFHC/AD, Delhi, 1990)

other ideologies like feminism and socialism insofar as they express class and women's interests and how these relate to the ideologies of communalism/religious fundamentalism.

The discussions were exploratory, raising more questions than answers, initiating a process in which we confronted ourselves and our context, at the same time as we identified external political/economic/cultural forces which had led to the emergence and acceleration of communal conflict and ethnic tension in the region. The issues we examined ranged from looking at the formation of the nation-state in each country and the dynamics of geopolitical relations within the region, to exploring the area of individual identities. This was further developed by examining the implications of identity politics within the women's movement in S.Asia in terms of its effects and future possibilities.

The nation-state and national identity

The definition of nationality — i.e. who and what makes one an Indian, Bangladeshi, Pakistani or Sri Lankan — becomes very complex especially as these definitions have shifted and changed over time and continue to do so today. It is difficult to reduce the basis of national identity to the lowest common denominator because this basis, whether it be religion, language or culture, tends to shift; other considerations assert themselves, both historically as well as at certain points in time. The S.Asian region has had strong anti-colonial movements, and in the early period after independence, Pakistan, India and Sri Lanka proclaimed secular national identities. However the national movement contained within itself different strands of nationalism — in Sri Lanka Sinhala nationalism, in India, Hindu and Muslim nationalism resulting in the creation of Pakistan, which itself is now subject to the assertion of linguistic nationalisms against the domination of Punjabi. The national movements thus carried within them communal/religious identities which, forty years after independence, all our nation-states have attempted to homogenise by forging a "national identity" in each country, papering over differences of religion, language and culture. This process of homogenisation however has tended to project one particular religion, language or ethnic group over the others. The process of forging a national identity has therefore been one of suppression and domination.

In Sri Lanka there was a shift from a more cosmopolitan/secular notion of national identity to a Sinhala-Buddhist national identity particularly after 1956. The control of state power by the Sinhala majority, the discrimination in education and employment against the Tamils and the increasing identification of the nation with a Sinhala-Buddhist identity led to the assertion of Tamil nationalism and the demand for a separate Tamil *eelam*. In Pakistan, an Islamic identity was imposed to ensure Punjab's economic and political domination over Sindhis, Baluchis and Pathans. The imposition of this particular identity as the Pakistani national identity was seen in the fact that the State had to continuously resort to violent suppression of other nationality struggles and minority sects through military force. In 1971 Bengali nationalism, based partly on linguistic identity and partly on the economic exploitation of East Pakistan by West Pakistan, led to the emergence of Bangladesh as a separate nation-state. Bengali nationalism, however, was also based on the suppression of other tribal and ethnic identities in Bangladesh. Today the State in Bangladesh is also attempting to forge an Islamic identity as the national identity. In India, the professed secular basis of a national identity has been eroded as the State is increasingly being identified with majority Hindu nationalism. There are questions being raised about whether the nation-state had ever, in fact, promoted a secular national identity. In the Punjab, there is a demand for a separate nation for the Sikhs and there has been an escalation of communal conflicts between Hindus/Muslims/Sikhs, with caste conflicts also being transformed into communal conflicts.

The basis for national identity has shifted within each country in the post-independence period with the religion, language or ethnicity of a dominant group emerging as well as being displaced at different conjunctures. The nation-state has sought to contain the effects of uneven capitalist development and the struggle for resources by different classes, by violent repression on the one hand and by attempting to impose a uniform, dominant-group national identity on the other. The attempt to impose a homogenous identity has been accompanied by the increasing centralisation of the State. Rooted in economic and political factors, there is today a deep crisis of nationalism and national identity in each country of the region.

While the State has sought to manipulate and impose a particular national identity, it is important to make a distinction between the nation-state and nationality. For example, in Bangladesh there was by and large, one major nationality which also constituted the nation-state although the tribals in the Chittagong Hill Tracts were seen, and continue to be viewed, as outsiders. In other countries of the region there were other nationalities within the nation-state. In Bangladesh being a Bengali meant being a Bangladeshi but in other countries such a conjunction is not easy to make. Even though the formation of this nation-state, like others in the region privileged certain characteristics as national and excluded others, at the same time it was felt that we had to be sensitive to historical experience, to the participation of people in Bangladesh,

हर एक आँख के आँसू हैं
अपनी पलकों में
हर एक सीने में
जो दर्द है, हमारा है

—फ़िराक़ गोरखपुरी

Rajasthan Kisan Sanghatana

for example, in forging a Bengali identity based on linguistic commonality as the national identity. The sharing of the literature of the language which, via the oral tradition, included sections of society who could not read, implied a qualitatively different formation. An issue which we did not explore further was whether language based nationalism has a more organic basis than religious nationalism and what implications this has for the formation of national identity.

Geopolitical dynamics - Indian hegemony in the region

There are many commonalities which link the region together as a distinct cultural entity. There exists a certain objective unity within the S. Asian region. Mohenjodaro, for instance, is part of a common historical past for Pakistan and India. As a result of colonial strategies and the emergence of new classes and developments in the colonial economy, there are now three separate nation-states in the subcontinent, along with Sri Lanka. Relations between these countries have varied from violent confrontation, as between India and Pakistan, to mutual exchange and alliances. One significant factor in the geopolitical dynamics of the region is the threat of Indian hegemony. The material basis of Indian hegemony rests on India's large military industrial complex. It has built up a manufacturing base in armaments which is different from other countries in the region. In addition, India also has a more developed indigenous capitalist class and it is the combination of economic and military strength which ensures Indian dominance within the region. (The Indian intervention in Sri Lanka through the IPKF has to be seen in this broader context as well.) This issue is closely linked with the question of whether Indian hegemony in the region is linked with an ideology of Hindu expansionism, i.e., is the Indian State a Hindu State today?

One could argue that if we examined the way modern Hinduism has emerged as a dominant, hegemonising ideology and the way it has spread over the subcontinent and was interpreted and used by colonialism, it does have the potential to become a state ideology as well. Hinduism has also been closely linked with Brahminism and has historically, supressed minority religious sects as well as lower castes and tribal communities. The selective construction of a "Syndicated Hinduism" by Hindu communal organisations today incorporates Brahminical values modelled on the linear structure of Semitic religions. This new Hinduism would also require a centralised, authoritarian state to impose its version onto the plurality and diversity of Indian society. These are areas which need further exploration. While it is crucial to establish whether the Indian State is in fact a Hindu State at the moment, the perception of this varies even within the country. There are many regional differences within India; while in the north one could clearly say that Hinduism is being projected as national ideology, in South India there is a difference, since Hindu communal parties like the BJP do not have a great influence in Tamil Nadu. Also the tradition of the anti-Brahmin movement has meant that while there are Hindu religions flourishing in the South, they are not primarily Brahminical. Similarly, there is a wide diversity and variation within Hinduism itself with numerous sects, caste groupings, etc., so that the internal diversity of Hinduism makes it difficult to assert one interpretation as the only one: the internal contradictions of Hinduism, particularly caste divisions may prevent the imposition of a particular Hinduism as the State ideology. The perception of Indian hegemony also varies according to countries; in Sri Lanka, for instance, hegemony in the region is seen as Indian, not Hindu, while in Pakistan the term "Indian expansionism" has a connotation of "Hindu" in it. Even in discussions within the Left in Pakistan these terms often become interchangeable, i.e., India= Hindu.

The basis of national identity has shifted and changed as a result of historical experiences and manipulation by the State, and regional, communal/ethnic identities often override a national identity. However there are moments when a national identity is asserted, particularly when an external other is seen as a threat. For instance war and cricket matches are two situations when a unified national identity is presented in opposition to the "enemy". This creation of a unified identity in opposition to an external other also makes for an assertion of a S. Asian identity; this occurs usually in confrontation with non-S.Asians abroad and is based on cultural factors like food, clothing, language and behavioral patterns. In such a context a regional S. Asian identity also gains validity. The articulation and assertion of different identities at different moments raises again the primary question of why people feel it is necessary to owe allegiance to these identities.

Communal identities : forced, imposed or chosen?

In trying to understand what made people respond to a communal identity we were entering uncharted territory. In particular the issue that concerned us was why women responded to a communal/fundamentalist identity when it was clearly retrogressive to their own interests as independent human beings. All individuals possess multiple identities and different ones come into play at different times. It becomes difficult to reduce an individual to one or two of these as *essential* to that person's total sense of being. The playing out of identities by individuals has to be seen in relation to biographical histories and

मन्दिर, मस्जिद, गुरुद्वारे ने बाँट लिया भगवान को
धरती बाँटी, सागर बाँटा, मत बाँटो इन्सान को

निशांत नाट्य मंच

social contexts. The expression of identity is negotiated in the space each individual finds between choice and the limitations determined by location (in time and space). Identities are therefore not primordial but are constantly being constructed and created as a result of individual, social and economic forces.

The mobilisation of certain identities involves different processes. In the context of communal/ethnic violence there are two processes at work which result in either forced identities or identities of affinity, i.e., those that are chosen on the basis of affinity. In either case both ideological and material factors play a role in this assertion. We felt it was important to examine both levels because communalism has been seen as only ideological even though the form it takes is material, as for instance, violence and the threat to economic survival. This perspective is important because in examining identities of affinity we find that people can choose either communal or non-communal ones. The fact of being a subordinated woman in a patriarchal society does not necessarily lead to a choice for a non-communal gender-or-class-based identity, since communal/ patriarchal identities also have a material basis in our societies. Alternative non-communal identifications therefore must also have a material base before they can become a social force in society.

At one level there are identities that are forced, i.e., not necessarily imposed through coercion but assumed because of a lack of choice in the given situation.

For example, the pressures of belonging to a minority community forced two Muslim women in India, Shehnaaz Sheikh and Shah Bano, to temporarily suspend taking up the issues of divorce and maintenance on secular grounds since the challenge to Muslim personal law was perceived as a threat to the whole identity of the Muslim community. It is in the context of power relations that particular identities are asserted. Although these two Muslim women had initially privileged their gender identity in demanding rights for women denied in Muslim personal law, the subsequent threat of Hindu domination forced them into placing their Muslim identity in the foreground. Another form of forced identity is seen in riot situations where, irrespective of an individual's political views or personal rejection of religion, s/he is seen as a Muslim/Hindu/Sikh/Buddhist or Christian. A similar process has occurred in Pakistan today where individuals are being classified in terms of their language and ethnic origins. As the S.Asian region becomes more and more polarised, the principle of exclusion and inclusion operates to reduce the space for the articulation of democratic, socialist, class or gender identities.

In examining identities of affinity, we felt that much more work had to be done on understanding why communal identities are chosen over others, particularly by women. Preliminary explorations have shown that women in religious fundamentalist organisations are not simply hegemonised by patriarchal ideology; their active involvement in these organisations has in fact freed them from traditional patriarchal controls over their mobility since they are allowed to move around in the service of god and the propagation and defence of their religion. Some younger women have also reported that they have been freed from the pressures of getting married since their lives are now seen to be valuable and legitimately engaged. Others have stated that involvement in fundamentalist groups has allowed them to participate in public life and have political discussions with men, again with the sanction of religion. These experiences have contradictory implications since the objective of many of these organisations is to restrict women to the home and family. However this does highlight the importance of examining the choice by women to support fundamentalism, in a more sensitive manner.

The women's movement or feminism as another identity of affinity has also been affected by the assertion of communal identities by women. For instance in Sri Lanka the women's movement was the first to take a public stand on the issue of autonomy for the Tamils in the North but this led to sharp divisions and splits, even among all the progressive groups. The Women's Action Committee split and only two or three groups are left. A new group called the Sinhala Women's Development Society was formed on chauvinist and nationalist lines.

मात्र अगर खामोश रहे
तो कल सन्नाटा छायेगा
हर बस्ती में आग लगेगी
हर बस्ती जल जायेगी
सन्नाटे के पीछे से तब
एक सदा ये आयेगी
कोई नहीं है कोई नहीं है
कोई नहीं है कोई नहीं

—साहिर लुधियानवी

Rajasthan Kisan Sanghatana

Subsequently more groups are being formed on the basis of ethnicity, particularly with the emergence of a Muslim political party. Another group called the Young Muslim Women's Association has recently emerged and is seen as fundamentalist. In India, too, separate Muslim women's groups have come into being. Many of them are not fundamentalist and are demanding changes within Muslim law, but they still feel the necessity to organise separately as Muslim women rather than as women per se on these issues. These developments in the women's movement in S.Asia have led to differences and raised a contradiction between the principle of autonomy, which is a basic principle of the movement, and the vision of uniting all women on the basis of a gender identity in a joint feminist movement. For example, on the one hand, Muslim women have the right to organise separately on their own issues; on the other, the formation of separate women's groups on the basis of religion in the context of communalism and rising fundamentalism could create dangerous splits. Although there have been class differences between women's organisations in S. Asia and the existence of separate women's organisations for women agricultural workers, contract workers, tribals and working women, there was little difference on issues, and joint struggles were launched by all the women's groups in support of even class-specific demands. The cross-class/caste mobilisation on demands and issues has been one of the major strengths of the women's movement in S.Asia. The escalation of communalism and ethnic divisions pose a threat to this unity. On the other hand the emergence of Muslim/Dalit feminist women's groups opens the possibility for new kinds of alliances.

Different strategies have been used to tackle these issues. One strategy has been to work within the terms of religious discourse and demand reforms within each religious group. Women's groups in Pakistan realised the dangers of this as they got trapped in a maze of interpretations of the Koran and finally ended up making the text the ultimate authority. This left little ground for them to oppose the final interpretation that was propagated. On the other hand the assertion of secular rights for women in India via the demand for a uniform civil code has also floundered. The demand has consistently been put forward by Hindu fundamentalists: Muslim women's groups have opposed it, and the autonomous women's movement has remained ineffective in acting on it.

One area that we were not able to discuss at all, even tentatively, was our own relationship to religion, as individual women, as feminists, and as a group meeting collectively. Not only is there no fully articulated position or discourse on religion by feminists in S.Asia, there is considerable ambivalence on the question of women and religion, per se, and on women, religion and feminism in particular.

At the level of the women's movement, our attempt has been to contain, as much as possible, the negative impact of religious practice and of fundamentalism on women, through campaigns against specific manifestations of both, with varying degrees of success. At the level of analysis, we have tried to establish the structural and systematic integration of religion with patriarchy, political economy and an increasingly powerful state in all our countries, and the consequences of this on women's subordinate status. In other words, we have sought to dispel the myth that religion today is merely a personal matter, consigned to the private domain. At the level of action, however, we have often been confounded by the place that religion occupies in most women's lives, and their relationship to religious and cultural practices that they find liberating; by the protest potential of religion itself; by the fact that many radical struggles in the region have been spearheaded by the church, for example; by the additional fact that, for many women, religion provides a sorely needed public space in which they find release from oppressive domesticity; and finally, that religious or ethnic collectivities are still a very powerful affinity group with which many of us identify, from time to time and under various circumstances, either for strategic reasons, or otherwise.

How problematic this relationship can be was reflected in our inability to a) adequately articulate a feminist concern with religion and, consequently, one aspect of identity politics; and b) articulate our own relationship to it, recognising that there was considerable diversity on this issue, even within this small group.

While specific strategies have to be evolved for confronting the combined forces of patriarchy/communalism and fundamentalism in the region, we felt that there were two areas in which the women's movement in S. Asia could link together and collaborate. A joint campaign on a charter of rights for women would move the issue of women's rights out of the discourse of personal laws with all its problems of communal identity. The fact that Muslim women in Pakistan, Bangladesh and Sri Lanka are also supporting this charter would support Muslim women in India, and women in Pakistan would get support in their demands for women's rights. In addition, broader issues of women s right and guarantee to work, of residence, etc., could be raised and this would broaden the struggle from its present focus on marriage, divorce and custody which are the areas covered by personal law.

The second is the effort to create an oppositional culture, a strengthening of support and resources within each women's movement so that, inspite of differences between women, it is possible to combine in action on major issues. An element of this oppositional culture is the spread of a S. Asian perspective where information, experiences and strategies are shared and a challenge made to attempts by the ruling parties in our countries to turn differences into divisions between countries and peoples.

The further development of a S. Asian perspective requires research, reflection and strategising around the following issues/questions:

1. The construction of the nation-state and nationality

In what ways did the construction of the post-colonial state incorporate particular notions of gender relations and women's position in society and the family? To what extent did these draw on colonial assumptions and practices? Which indigenous traditions were selected to forge an anti-colonial nationalism and what were the notions of womanhood projected as representing national models? What were the dominant categories used in the projection of national models of womanhood and what were the shifts and tensions within these? What was responsible for shifts in this model — for example, in Bengali nationalism from the vengeful Kali to the gentle Durga, from the militant fighter to mothers and wives as upholders of harmony? Did the large-scale participation of women in the national movements lead to any transformation in these notions of womanhood? What alternative models of gender relations were articulated and by which groups? Did the delineation of national boundaries include a particular definition of gender relations? Does language-based nationalism have more progressive implications for women than religion-based nationalism? What are the factors which have led linguistic nationalisms into becoming religious/ fundamentalist/ nationalist movements?

2. The post-colonial state, capitalist development and cultural identity

Given the commitment at varying levels to secularism and equal rights by all independent nation-states, what were the reasons for changes in state ideology on these issues? How far was the space for such shifts already present in the structure of the colonial and post-colonial state, which attempted to balance communal representation and secularism? How far do class, caste and gender form a material basis for identities in S. Asia? Is there a national identity or a regional identity in S. Asia today? What are the ideological and material factors which have led to the mobilisation of communal/ethnic identities? What are the implications of populism for women? What are the material factors which can lay the basis for a non-communal gender identity? In what ways has the assertion of a gender identity through feminism been affected by fundamentalist assertions of gender identity? What examples are there in our histories of group/community identities with a democratic ideology?

3. Women as objects and subjects of fundamentalist discourse

What are the commonalities in the discourse on gender between different fundamentalist movements? Is it possible to arrive at a universal definition of fundamentalism? How far are these movements different in their conceptualisation and actions on gender relations from revivalist and reformist religious movements? What are the factors which have led women to join fundamentalist organisations? How do women themselves relate to communal/fundamentalist ideologies? What are the means through which women are co-opted by fundamentalist movements? Are there contradictions between the personal and political space provided to these women within fundamentalist movements and the restrictions demanded for women by fundamentalists? What are the common features between the feminist and fundamentalist critique of capitalism? How has the Left responded to fundamentalism and feminism?

And, finally, in the light of a growing alliance between right-wing economics and right-wing politics, which is the ground that women occupy?

Shamshad

In defence of our secular tradition

कहीं रामदास कहीं फते मुहम्मद,
यही क़दीमी शोर ।
मुसलमान चिता से चिढ़ते,
हिन्दू चिढ़ते गोर ।
ख़त्म हुए सब झगड़े रगड़े,
निकल पड़ा कोई और ।

- बुल्ले शा

SAHMAT
8, Vitthalbhai Patel House,
Rafi Marg, New Delhi 110 001
Ph: 3711276

Gender (ed) struggles: the state, religion and civil society

Shahnaz J. Rouse

Amili Setalvad

This paper analyses the nature of the Pakistani State, focusing on its interaction with religious forces, with a view to understanding the impact of this relationship on women in Pakistani society. Although this essay draws on the Pakistani experience, its themes and conceptual approach are by no means limited to that context and can be extended to an examination of women's issues in other countries in the Islamic world.

The role of religion in women's subordination

In recent years a rich literature has developed around the relationship of gender and ideology. Many feminists in the Muslim world have specifically taken up the issue of women and religion. Writers such as Fatima Mernissi, Nawal el Saadawi, Farah Azari, Leila Ahmad, Azar Tabari and Nahid Yahganeh are but a few.[1] They have been among the forerunners in questioning the nature of the relationship between gender construction, religion(focusing on Islam) and society. I will draw upon their general scholarship in this area to indicate the manner in which gender and ideology (specifically religious ideology) are interrelated socially, culturally and historically.

There are two broad levels at which religion intersects with society and consequently affects women's location, status and opportunities. First, and most pervasive, is the role religion plays in constructing gender at the level of culture. This is the arena of civil society. Second, there is the level of the national polity whereby religion is deployed as an institutional force in policy formulation, dissemination and implementation. These two levels, the cultural and the political, are not isolated from and independent of each other; but for analytical purposes, I would like to treat each of these contexts separately.

At the cultural level, religion informs our notions of sexuality, marriage, the family, appropriate roles, work and so on. These aspects of everyday life are all too often taken for granted and seldom subjected to close scrutiny. Yet it is precisely here that the socialisation of both men and women as individual agents has been rooted, historically; and it is these continuities, as well as the discourses and institutions that reproduce these practices that must be challenged if systemic changes are to be achieved in women's status and social location.

This should not be read as an assertion that cultural notions and constructions of gender inequality are either monolithic, universal and/or trans-historical. It is almost banal to state that there have always existed dominant and competing cultures on the same geographical terrain. Similarly, socio-economic realities constantly serve to modify and transform cultural modalities over time. Increased education, harsh economic conditions whereby women's relation to work is transformed, are but two realities which serve to shake up the cultural milieu as it pertains to women.

These changes do not automatically result in a necessary and parallel transformation in popular perceptions regarding women's role and position in society. Consider, for a moment, Pakistani official statistics which continue to under-represent women's labour force participation and contribution. Also consider the example of the Iranian revolution which has attempted, if not to banish women from the work force entirely, then to allocate them a distinct position so that they are once again segregated and rendered subservient to men.

At the level of national polity, the relationship between religion and the State reflects the configuration of political forces that exist within a given social formation at any particular time and the relative strength of existing political groups. The strength of religious elements is directly related to the weakness of bourgeois and left forces at any particular conjuncture.

Within Muslim societies, however (and Pakistan is no exception), it is at the level of the national polity that the cultural and political forces intersect in a particular and peculiar fashion.[2] Arguing that the early Islamic state did not make a separation between state and religion, certain religious groups have mounted a major offensive against contemporary state formations wherein their role has been diminished. These same forces have played a crucial role in laying claim to and invariably asserting control over, precisely those elements of state policy that pertain to women. Rules governing the faimily — marriage, inheritance, divorce — have legally been conceded, in Pakistan as in many other Muslim countries, as the preserve of religious authorities and a particularly constituted religious morality.[3]

This has two consequences. First, in areas where women have most immediately been subordinated, such as the family, the discourse has been conducted predominantly within religious parameters. With rare exceptions,[4] any legal changes that have been introduced with respect to women have been changes of degree not of essence,and are always susceptible to reversal. This also means that when women demand legal changes or legal equality, they must directly confront religious authority and institutions. In societies where Islamic fundamentalism is experiencing a resurgence, consequent upon the failure of the bourgeois elements and of the left, this means not just a cultural confrontation but a political one as well.

Islamic fundamentalism and the Pakistani State

The Pakistani State and Muslim religious forces have existed in a complicated and contradictory relationship from the very inception of the country. At the time of the anti-colonial movement, Muslim religious elements in India were deeply divided. The nationalists and pan-Islamist elements either supported the secular Indian National Congress and/or joined the Khilafat movement as a means of opposing colonial rule.[5] Those religious elements that were later to move to Pakistan and constitute the Jamaat-i-Islami under Maulana Maudoodi's leadership, strenuously and vehemently opposed the notion of a separate Pakistan.[6] Their primary

Amili Setalvad

objection was to the Muslim League leadership which they accused of being "secular", aping the west, and thereby charged with collaboration and inauthenticity. Complicating their vision was their resistance to modern nationalism. They posited nationalism as being in opposition to "Islamic universalism" which was held to transcend national frontiers and boundaries. Another concern centered around the status of Muslims who would be left behind in an independent India. These issues led to vocal and sustained propaganda against the very idea of Pakistan, including the designation by some among the opponents of the Pakistan Movement's leader, Jinnah, as kafir (unbeliever).

Once Pakistan achieved independence, a number of these oppositional religious elements migrated to Pakistan. Under Maudoodi's leadership, the Jamaat-i-Islami directed all its efforts towards political activity. Its goal became the annihilation of a prospective secular Pakistan and the establishment, in its stead, of an Islamic theocracy within the country; not a country of Muslims (as Jinnah had postulated), but a Muslim country.[7] By definition, this meant their active involvement at both the political and cultural levels.

Thus politics has guided the Islamic fundamentalists from the very inception of Pakistan in 1947. Their stated goals, coalitions formed, ideological positions taken, have all been directed towards developing a political base and ultimately acquiring political hegemony. Since 1947, they have contested elections at all levels. They have also pursued a systematic policy of infiltrating educational and government institutions, with a view to eventually taking over state power and they are also cognizant of the need to disseminate their ideas throughout civil society.[8]

Interestingly, religious ideologues (especially those connected with religiously-based political parties) have been singularly unsuccessful throughout Pakistan's short history in gaining much of a mass base when it comes to electoral politics. This inability to gain a foothold in national politics through the ballot box explains their tactic of working from within the bureaucracy and military in order to entrench themselves within the state apparati: what they could not achieve through elections they would attempt through anti-democratic means.

The possibility of acquiring state power in this fashion did eventually materialise. When Zia came to power through the military coup that deposed Bhutto and the Pakistan People's Party, the Jamaat was present and ready to collaborate with his regime. Indeed, many Pakistanis insist that the Jamaat was a key player in precipitating both Bhutto's downfall and encouraging the military takeover.[9] This collaboration enabled them to realise their long sought-after goal as co-partners, if not direct masters, in state power.

The reasons for this transformation following the military coup in 1977 are multiple. The Jamaat already had individuals in positions of power in state institutions who could play a role in determining policy, now that formal democracy had been set aside. Additionally, Zia desperately needed ideological allies, especially to justify his postponement of elections. This the fundamentalists could, and were, eager to be: their experience with elections had impressed upon them that this was one avenue through which they could not gain access to state power.[10]

In order to understand the continued significance of Islamic ideology and discourse beyond Zia-ul Haq's period, we need to turn our attention to a key issue: the failure (indeed it might be more appropriate to say shallowness) of bourgeois politics and modernist ideology in Pakistan. While stemming from a complicated historical process but unique in its specific local manifestations, this failure can be traced to two separate yet related factors: first, the underdeveloped nature of the bourgeois class as a whole and its subsequent inability to establish its hegemony over the State. This has meant that in order to maintain its economic privilege, the bourgeoisie in Pakistan as elsewhere in the Third World, has been all too willing to relinquish its political power to the military, and anti-democratic forces. Second, and related to the weakness of the bourgeoisie itself, a reliance on a discourse of universalism that undermines the claims of oppressed social strata including workers (rural and urban), ethnic and religious minorities, and women.[11]

The rise of fundamentalism in Pakistan is therefore directly related to the inability of the bourgeois class to rule. This in turn results from the problems attendant upon class dynamics, political and economic, in the context of peripheral societies where

Communalism Combat

economic growth is highly dependent and political power unconsolidated among the dominant classes.

It is also the refraction of the tensions that accompany national development and social change in Third World societies which are restrained structurally from adopting an independent road to change and thus, not infrequently through local bourgeois agency, wittingly or unwittingly become pawns in the imperialist agenda for global hegemony.[12] In the Pakistani context there is a peculiar twist to this last reality. Unlike Iran, where the fundamentalists gained popular support by becoming the paramount institutional force through which opposition was channelled,[13] in Pakistan the fundamentalists acquired access to state power by overthrowing a popularly elected regime. This means that the equation in Pakistan is the opposite of the Iranian one. The consequences of this difference are critical.[14]

Another factor that distinguishes the Pakistani experience from other peripheral societies resides in the very premise for its existence. Pakistan is one of two countries in the world (the other being Israel) that relied on religion as the raison d'etre of its being. Even though many Pakistanis argue that Pakistan today is not what its proponents envisioned, this position fails to analytically incorporate a critical understanding of the inherent weakness in religious difference as a basis for nation formation. It holds the potential of future reliance on it both for identity formation and as a unifying force, further compounded when the State fails to address the basic needs of its oppressed peoples. Given the structural imperative to reproduce existing relations of inequality, religion becomes the basis for nationalism, a symbol of "oneness". Conveniently, the otherness of the imperialising metropole further serves this construction in the context of a state that defines itself as "Muslim", and in pursuit of "authentic" development.[15] Such constructions serve to gloss over existing structures of difference that are internal to civil society and its related structures, and justify such glossing over in the name of an idealised identity.

What has this alliance between religious ideology and the Pakistani State meant for women? One area that has always been of immediate concern to fundamentalists has been that of family laws. Under the Zia regime, the gains women had made in this realm, however insignificant, came under attack. Not only were previously won rights brought into question but the scope of Shariat law has been vastly extended. Thus new laws of evidence and retribution have been promulgated which promise to create an environment in which women are adversely affected, for all venues are under challenge — dress, choice in marriage, divorce, inheritance, education, and so on.

The collaboration between the fundamentalist religious forces and the State

has altered since Benazir Bhuttto and, later, Nawaz Sharif came to power. This change however does not constitute a break from the past but a further consolidation of trends most blatantly visible during the Zia regime.[16] While religious ideas and control over family policy are still in place, religious authorities no longer occupy a central position in the institutions of state or the political process. Instead the new middle class, which began to evolve in the 1960s and grew enormously after 1977, is formally ensconced in power, working in close collaboration and cooperation with elements of the military and religious groups.

It is my contention that what we have seen in Pakistan is a contestation among different factions of the intermediate strata for control over the State.[17] Religious ideology has been implicated in this struggle from the country's very inception although different factions have attempted to define themselves and their opponents distinctly.[18]

Seen thus, Zia's regime and the coming to power of the fundamentalists can be re-visioned as a logical outcome of processes started much earlier — ideologically at the time of independence and prior, economically, at the inception of Ayub Khan's development decade. Thus it is the crisis of the peripheral state and its continued imperialist alliances that help explain Islamic resurgence in Pakistan. The repression of non-religious oppositional groups helped strengthen the possibilities for such an outcome.

The post-colonial Pakistani State has had to wrestle with a weak bourgeoisie and has resorted to the construction of a centralised state apparatus as a necessary corollary to continued capitalist control in the economic realm. In doing so, it has also changed in constitutional and discursive directions: today, that segment of the middle class that emerged through state patronage under Zia and in the course

of the development process initiated in the 1960s holds sway, having successfully displaced those who previously held power. With a brief interlude under
Benazir (during which period she too was unable and/or unwilling to dislodge this new strata completely), Nawaz Sharif's regime saw the maturation
of a process initiated much earlier.

In this transition, Nawaz Sharif's regime continued to rely on an Islamic
ideology whereby justifications were sought for the repression of subordinated groups, women being paramount among those targetted. The rhetoric
of "Pakistani nationalism" and its accompanying modernisation policies having previously been discredited, religious discourse constitutes a powerful
substitute.[19] In my opinion it is a curious irony that given the way capitalism
and civilisational identities have been constituted historically, even progressive forces within Pakistan frequently collapse the former into the latter,
thereby blunting any critique of economic structures in systemic, structural
terms. In doing so they play right into the hands of groups proposing religion
and civilisational categories as causative and explanatory variables in understanding history.[20]

In noting the above dynamics, it is critical that one deepen the analysis so as
not to render it one-sided and unproblematic. Not only do these developments
exist in a contradictory relationship to on-going socio-economic transforma-
tions insofar as they impact upon women, the tensions express themselves
within the State itself.

Women and socio-economic transitions

In the forty-odd years since Pakistan's independence, there has been a pro-
found shift in the class structure of Pakistani society. This shift from a formal to
a real subsumption of labour under capital which began under Ayub acquired
political centrality during Zia's regime.[21]

The most significant outcome of developmental trends, for the present
discussion, is the emergence of a transformed and expanded middle class,
which is now centrally positioned both economically and politically. The very
process and policies of development in the country — the green revolution
and accompanying agrarian reform, overseas labour migration and state patronage — have contributed to its creation. This class has several faces: professional (contingent upon educational privilege and/or patronage); a rural or
urban strata engaged in non-productive activities (wholesalers and retailers);
and agro-based small manufacturing. While these processes detrimentally
affected large sections of the population and adversely impacted different
regional groups, they also led, simultaneously, to the enlargement of the

petty bourgeoisie.

Recent analyses by Hamza Alavi and Arif Hasan focus on the significance of this new development within the class structure of Pakistan.[22] Consistent factors in Pakistan's economy over the last decade and a half have been an inflationary economy predicated on the availability of funds produced in the informal sector, remittances by overseas workers, money from drug trafficking, and huge doses of foreign aid. A substantial part of the growth of this middle class thus lies outside the productive economy. Women's location within this middle class is essentially contradictory, and it is this contradiction we must address in gauging women's circumstances.

Let me make two general points with respect to class and gender. First, the process of development undertaken in Pakistan has tended to exacerbate regional differences. This variation has critical implications for gender relations and women's location in different parts of the country. Thus women in the tribal areas are situated differentially from those living within the system in Baluchistan.[23] Tribal gender relations in turn differ from those in urban centres and in settled agricultural areas.

Second, class differences directly impact on women in a fashion that differentiates among them and informs their sense of self. In other words, women of all classes do not experience their subordination identically. In this analysis, I will focus primarily on settled agricultural areas and on urban centres.

Capital penetration into agriculture has had a disparate effect on women. The very character of combined and uneven development has made it impossible for the economy to see a universalisation of particular forms of production and social relations.[24] While the tendency in rural areas is towards increased proletarianisation, the process is uneven.

In some areas women are forced to enter the paid labour force, in others they are pushed out of production. The former occurs in areas where mechanisation is incomplete, or where women serve as a cheap source of seasonal labour. They tend to get pushed out in those areas where mechanisation is complete and cheap labour no longer a necessity, the requirement being instead for a permanent technical and managerial staff.

Despite these differences, there is one uniform tendency: rural women, who have historically been part of the labour force, must now double their efforts to reproduce the domestic unit. Government statistics have consistently under-reported women's productive contribution; they do not therefore accurately reflect the additional burden imposed on women in recent times. More criti-cally, with the shift from subsistence to cash production, households are thrown into the market economy. The need for cash has forced women and men to seek alternative means of employment when traditional sources are lost. Women have not necessarily retired from work; rather they have been forced into alternative jobs.

Another change that has transpired in the rural economy is that certain groups have benefitted from the process of transformation. Large landlords, as well as certain artisans and other rural strata, through connections and/or wage employment were able to establish themselves as rural entrepreneurs. While some of these households hire-in wage labour, others engage in petty commodity production using family labour only. Their drive is towards ex-pansion. Another group in evidence in areas where capitalisation of agricul-ture has intensified is connected to small-scale agro-based industrial production, servicing agricultural machinery.

The rural economy has also been altered by migration overseas. This has resulted in labour shortages, and remittances used primarily for investment in land and property. Among migrant families, some writers have argued that openings have emerged for women given that they now have to manage family affairs.[25] Thus it is assumed that they have been liberated from male control. My own findings suggest that this is debatable. Women's subordina-tion rests not merely on the presence of immediate male kin (husbands, fathers, brothers), but is reproduced through a much wider system of *biradari* ties. Making assumptions rather than examining post-migration gender rela-tions also evades the question of women's own complicity in maintaining certain patterns of gendered behaviour; and lastly, it begs the question as to what transpires once the migrating male returns: are new social relations fostered among the two sexes, or do men attempt to reassert control through returning to prior patterns?

To understand the constraints and liberatory influences relevant to gender construction one must look beyond class relations.There are two distinct strands within the urban middle class. At one end are the professionals, at the other women within the "traditional" middle class, segregated and confined to domestic work. Between these two extremes are positioned women engaged in the "putting-out" system who work either under the direction of their husbands (or other male family members), or else operate within a collective operation, organised and run by women. Home-based work may also function under the control of an entrepreneur from outside the family, in which case the women would operate as paid wage workers.[26] In other words, while the location of work is the same in all instances, the relation to work varies enormously depending on the way it is structured, as does the self-perception among the women concerned.

An integral part of the urban working class are women who serve as domestics, industrial workers, and as members of the informal sector in a variety of capacities. Bourgeois women in the urban sector, like their rural counterparts, are by definition members of the leisure class who rely on domestics to take care of household tasks. Clearly women in the urban economy are highly differentiated in terms of their insertion into discrete systems of social and work relations. My contention is that the middle class constitutes the crucial strata for reasons I will now attempt to explicate.

Educated middle class women are increasingly entering the labour force. While many scholars rationalise this incorporation on grounds of necessity, I would argue that, for at least a small (but expanding) proportion, it is also a matter of choice. More educated women than ever before are opting for a professional life over their traditionally circumscribed role as housewives. Insistence on necessity as the grounds for this shift accomplishes two things: first, it validates women's primary role as homemakers and privileges "the family" as a natural and/or inevitable social unit. Second, it ultimately suggests disapproval should a woman choose not to marry and exercise the option to work instead. Thus scholars and activists sympathetic to women are quick to point out that women work *only* because they *must*; while others are equally quick to point out that these women are privileged and therefore cannot possibly address issues relevant to most (other) Pakistani women. Such logic is flawed, regardless of whether it originates from the left or right. Ultimately, it reproduces notions of normalcy of women's position within the household as nurturers and caretakers. It continues to operate within the broader framing of the issue of gender that denies agency to women, except insofar as they strive to `better' the family. It also potentially provides the basis for reaction against all women who work outside the home.

Lesser educated women among this class might work as nurses, in public schools, and other institutions in the public and private sector, but unlike the previous group, they do not have the support of a network of established urban connections. Because of this they are exposed to work-related sexual harassment and greater economic insecurity.

It is among women deprived of education or with minimal schooling that inflationary trends, combined with migration to the cities, operate most strongly to affect as well as inhibit choices. It is also within this group that their status as "economically active workers" goes unrecognised.[27] This results not only from biases in statistical compilation and definitions of "productive" labour, but more significantly, from perceived social stigma attached to women's employment,per se. This prevents admissions regarding one's family members working for "strangers". Denied access to more "respectable" professional jobs, these women have little recourse but to engage in home-based work either for themselves, male family members, or agents who organise and market the output of a network of women.

From the cursory examination just completed, we can clearly see the heterogeneous implications of this development process depending on diverse class positions occupied by women. Women are caught in the interstices of this contradictory process. *Necessity* and the need for *respectability* further inhibit women's ability to re-position themselves in the work arena. In this regard progressives and fundamentalists are unwitting allies: the former use the logic of modernism, the nation, or the larger good, while the latter insist on religious principle, modesty and community. Such insistence and justification serve as the basis of self-identification for fundamentalist women and constitutes the marker of separation from those *other*, non-respectable women — the professionals (dubbed as *westernised*) — and also working class women who are cast as the objects of pity and /or contempt.[28]

A discourse exists around women and work that distinguishes *respectable* from *non-respectable* work, respectable from non-respectable *reasons for work*, and respectable from non-respectable *women*. It is this construction that sets the terms of the debate on women's labour force participation, and at least in part, helps explain their complicity in the reproduction of their subordinate status. In a society where women's status and social (as opposed to economic) privilege resides in their virtue, the latter's protection becomes a paramount concern not only among the men of the household but among women themselves. Not only does this operate significantly with regard to control over women's bodies and sexuality, it is of manifest significance in the visibility/invisibility of women's labour force participation.

The State, too, is caught within these warring tendencies. It must simultaneously strive to appease international agencies and donors insistent on a *women's component in development* projects, realise the fruits of its own modernising projects, as well as reproduce its ideological stance on unity of identity and ideas. Regardless of the State's desire it should be clear that a space exists through the processes described within which women can challenge the orthodoxy and status quo.

The location of women's struggles and issues of women's rights

The reconstruction of the basis of Pakistani identity and nationality gained renewed vigour following the military takeover in 1977 and the alliance between fundamentalists and the State. The space created permitted conservative religious groups to adopt a virulently anti-feminist stance; it also led to changes in laws pertaining to women and to increased violence against them, political, class-based, and social.[29] Since 1981, women have been engaged in a visible struggle against such state policies that jeopardise their status and position in society. The resistance has used a variety of forms —organisational, literary, scholarly, etc.

In 1981 the Women's Action Forum, in conjunction with other women's groups, using a diversity of means — petitions, media exposure, conferences, seminars, demonstrations, etc. — attempted to put pressure on Zia's (and later Nawaz Sharif's) regime to alter their positions. Short term victories resulted on specific issues but overall attempts to overturn and indeed to prevent laws pertaining to women from being changed negatively, have been largely unsuccessful.

This initiative did, however, see some gains. First, it drew sympathy and support from many segments of the population who felt deprived and re-pressed by Zia's regime in particular. This helped raise the level of awareness and concern about women's issues in Pakistan in a manner previously unpar-alleled.

It also brought the issue of women's oppression to the attention of all political parties, and at least for a while ensured that all opposition parties addressed the issue on their party platforms. This still holds true for most social democratic and progressive groups.

Third, the visibility and achievements of WAF demonstrated the potential for struggle. Since WAF was engaged in anti-State activities under Zia, it not only created a space for women, it also demonstrated that an oppositional space could be carved out even under an extremely repressive regime. In that sense, WAF stood at the forefront of progressive politics during the Zia era.

Since then however, WAF has ceased to occupy centre-stage in the women's struggle for change. Other groups, such as Sindhiani Tehrik, have emerged in the political field. What is noticeable in Pakistan today is the enormous mush-rooming of groups involved with issues of concern to women. Many of these have chosen to take direct advantage of the contradictions within the State itself and have sought funding for their efforts either by constituting them-selves as non-governmental organisations or as consulting groups funded by international agencies and / or the State. These groups are engaged not only in research and action projects relevant to women, but also in subsidising publications on women's literary, social and legal status. More individual women have entered the political process as a result of this experience. Through these shifts, the women's struggle in Pakistan today is no longer restricted to issues that only pertain to a few women or to reforms that can be taken advantage of by a few privileged women.[30] In the current phase fundamental issues, such as crimes against women, are being raised and addressed in a concerted fashion.

In terms of the possibilities for women's rights to be acceded, it should by now be clear that this question belongs essentially to the realm of democratic and human rights. Many Pakistanis argue that Pakistan has still not experienced a return to democratic rule, despite the fact that both Benazir Bhutto and Nawaz Sharif came to power through elections. Given the fragility and incompleteness of the democratic process in Pakistan, and the failure of bourgeois politics, the only groups with a long-term stake in the institutionalisation of such rights are the most depressed strata, that is the producing classes. These are also the only classes capable of creating a genuine democracy in the Pakistani context. It is to an alliance with these classes that women must turn if they are to ensure their rights, but this is by no means an easy task. Many of the women in the leadership of the current Pakistani women's movement come from the more affluent sections. There is, therefore, an in-built tension between their class and gender location. This makes it possible for the State and those opposed to women's rights to play off the class position of women activists against the gender interests that tie them to other women. Only by broadening their base and democratising their organisational structures whereby local groups can exercise local leadership will these two hurdles be overcome.

An even more critical imperative, in my opinion is for women to challenge nationality politics. A history of nationalism in peripheral states in general indicates that it was always predicated on a prior subordination of women to a larger cause rendering the question of women's rights secondary. In Pakistan, this scenario is repeated but with

an even more troublesome twist: women's subordinate status is relegated to divine sanction by virtue of fundamentalist religious ideology. Thus, the women's movement must not only broaden its base in class terms but also deny primacy to any form of nationalism since all versions — religious, ethnic, class — rest on privileging one oppression over others. In order to succeed, women must insist on the interrelatedness of different forms of oppression. The semantic recognition of exploitation as distinct from oppression cannot be used as justification for privileging struggles against the former system over the latter.

In the Pakistani context, as long as religion continues to be interlinked with the State, any gains achieved under that structure will, at best, be tangential, transitory and incomplete. Not because religion as such is at fault, but because any attempt at religious hegemony necessarily negates the validity of alternative belief systems.

Not only is there a need to lift discourses on women out of the sanctified realm of religion and custom, the heterogeneous character of belief systems needs to be stressed and its material bases noted. To do otherwise, in any multi-religious society is to invite disaster for one sector of society or another. Ironically, it is this recognition of difference that will permit a realisation of true humanity and its accompanying universalism.

Formal democratic rights, while a necessary progression, must be understood as merely one step (limited at that) in the direction of women's liberation. Struggles for such rights must be accompanied by struggles at the cultural level where gender ideology is most deeply entrenched. This means that women begin to address issues which are undoubtedly extremely sensitive. These include questions of sexuality, and the role of the family in gender socialisation. These areas are only just beginning to emerge. The recent attempt by Pakistani feminists to forge a link with women researching these questions in other Muslim countries is a necessary and important beginning. The agenda is enormous and the scope of work immense. Pakistani women in the 1980s have shown courageous beginnings; they now need to build on the promise of radically transforming their own position and redefining society as well.

Notes

This article is a synthesis as well as an amended and extended version of two previously published articles which appeared first in *Pakistan Progressive* and later in *South Asia Bulletin*.

1   Leila Ahmed, *Women and Gender in Islam: Historical Roots of a Modern Debate* (New Haven: Yale University Press, 1992); Fatima Mernissi, *Beyond the Veil: Male-Female Dynamics in*

Modern Muslim Society (Bloomington: Indiana University Press, 1987): Nawal el Saadawi, *The Hidden Face of Eve* (London: Zed Press, 1986); Azar Tabari and Nahid Yahgeneh, *In the Shadow of Islam* (London: Zed Press, 1983).

2 It is at the level of the State that religious ideology gets cast into policy. The capacity of this ideology to be asserted more or less forcefully is dependent on various factors, including (but by no means limited to) the ideology of the regime in power, hegemony or lack thereof of the regime, and the relative strength of organised fundamentalist groups.

3 Religious authorities have been singularly unsuccessful in bringing about major policy changes in the economic realm. Thus, *ushr*, the Islamic agrarian tax, was never implemented in Pakistan. Even struggle around it was abandoned early on in the Zia period. Similarly, changes in interest- bearing accounts (given the prohibition against usury in Islam), have been semantic and procedural rather than susbstantive.

4 One exception was Turkey under Ataturk, who completely abolished religious law and introduced total secularisation in the legal realm. This included family law. Whether these laws actually succeeded in transforming the overall cultural milieu with respect to women is a separate matter.

5 Maulana Abul Kalam Azad is one of the best known Islamic theologians of this period. His book *India Wins Freedom* (Bombay: Orient Longman, 1964), discusses the viewpoint of those Muslims who opted for a united India.

6 Maulana Maudoodi was known for his vehement opposition to the very notion of Pakistan. His deepest disdain was reserved for Jinnah whom he mockingly called Kafir-e-Azam (a take-off on the title conferred on him by supporters of the Pakistan Movement, Quaid-e-Azam). Given this opposition it is little wonder that, immediately after independence, Maudoodi found little sympathy or support among Pakistani nationalists or its bourgeois class.

7 Jinnah's vision was of a secular Pakistan in which Muslims constituted a majority but where the civil rights of minorities were to be protected and guaranteed by the Constitution.

8 See I.A. Rehman, "Jamat: The Politics of Religion", *Herald*, September 1987; and "A Fundamental Dilemma", *Herald*, October 1987.

9 The PNA coalition led the demonstrations against the last elections in which Bhutto won, just prior to his downfall. There is also widespread commentary within Pakistan that supports the notion of an alliance between the perpetrators of the coup against Bhutto and fundamentalist forces.

10 This was most evident in the access to the mass media by fundamentalists during and since Zia's regime; by the establishment of a Majlis-e-Shoora (Religious Council); by the visibility and increased powers of Shariat courts.

11 In Pakistan, universalist discourses have necessarily been hedged by other discursive strains that contradict their claims. Thus the claim of a secular constitutional state, on the western model, was contradicted by the very logic that led to Pakistan's existence: its rationale as a country of, even if not for, Muslims.

12 Control by international capital in collusion with the comprador classes internal to the society, the latter striving to implement a "modernisation" agenda, has often led to an emphasis on insider/outsider dichotomies and on form rather than structure.

13 This is not to argue that the anti-Shah movement was organised and conducted solely by religious elements; all accounts suggest that the left and other social groupings were an integral part of the struggle. I am suggesting that, given the degree of repression meted out to other groups, they could not have operated in as cohesive a fashion as the religious forces. Since the latter continued to have access to mosques, they were able to mobilise people and take control of the movement.

14 Since the Iranian revolution was perceived as an anti-imperialist , anti-monarchical struggle, the Ayatollahs were able to amass popular support. In Pakistan, on the other

hand, given the role the mullahs played in deposing a populist regime with a popular leader at its helm, the fundamentalists actually lost respect among vast sections of working Pakistanis subsequent to the change of regime.

[15] "Authentic" development emphasises culture over economics; form over substance; the appearance of exploitation over its underlying structural essence. To the extent that the personae of internal and external capitalism can be seen as culturally different, collapsing economics into cultural icons and images is eminently feasible and a potent tool. What is interesting is that in the process of bringing about this displacement, Islam itself becomes reified and transformed into a static and fixed entity, rather than being understood as differentially and historically constituted through interpretation and revision.

[16] To date, there has been no major work tracing this continuity. Piecemeal analyses have been undertaken, largely in Pakistani newspapers and news journals such as *Herald*, *Viewpoint* and *Newsline*.

[17] This idea is borrowed from Aijaz Ahmad's article "Class, Nation and State: Intermediate Classes in Peripheral Societies", published in Dale L. Johnson (ed.), *Middle Classes in Dependent Countries* (Beverly Hills: Sage Publications, 1985), pp.43-66.

[18] See my article, "Discourses on Gender in Pakistan: Convergence and Contradiction"' in D. Allen (ed.), *Religion and Political Conflict in South Asia* (Greenwood Press), forthcoming.

[19] Here I am referring to the manner in which the Pakistani ideology of one nation, with Punjabis in power, was challenged first by the Bengalis, and later by the Baluch and Sindhis. In class terms, the failure of the ruling classes' modernising project has been linked to their failed political project.

[20] For a discussion of the historical dimension of Islamic ideas and practices in one social realm— that of sexuality—see the works of Leila Ahmed and Nahid Yahganeh.

[21] This refers to the Marxian notion that in an earlier phase of capitalism, old forms(that is social relations) remain in place while undergoing a shift in their underlying logic. It is only at a later stage that the forms themselves are replaced by social relations clearly based on a separation of the worker from the product as well as from the means of production. In the Pakistani context, the latter process was intensified under Ayub Khan but deepened even further in the late 1970s and early 1980s.

[22] See Hamza Alavi, "Pakistani Women in a Changing Society", mimeo; and Arif Hasan, "Day of the Middleman", *Herald*, November 1989.

This is not to argue that the same individuals continue to occupy this middle strata. It is evident that large segments of the rural middle peasantry have lost their position and joined the proletariat. In other words, just as there is a definitive sliding downward of large numbers of households which previously occupied a position in the middle strata, there is a simultaneous upward mobility among other households which have benefitted from the economic and political processes detailed out. What is most significant, however, is the increased access by this new middle class to the institutions and apparati of the State.

[23] This recognises the fact that the tribal structures of the two regions are not identical. Ethnographic studies reveal the distinct differences making for the varieties of positions which women occupy.

[24] For a theoretical treatment of such differences and their underlying logic see Michael Lowy, *Combined and Uneven Development* (London: Verso, 1977).

[25] Fareeda Shaheed, in a study conducted for the International Labor Organisation in a *barani* village named Jhok Sayal makes this assertion. In a village in Shahpur Tehsil where I conducted fieldwork between 1979-82, and again in 1985, there was only one family in which the head of household had gone overseas to work. However, a married son had taken over the father's position as patriarch.

[26] This information is largely drawn from Hamza Alavi, *op.cit.*

[27] My own doctoral research points to the high percentage of women actively engaged in

productive activities in the rural sector. These findings are corroborated by research done by the Women's Action Forum and Shirkat Gah. There are several factors that combine to distort women's productive contribution: first, whenever surveys are conducted, they rely on male informants who interview and collect information largely from other men. Second, most men are unwilling to acknowledge work done by women because of the social stigma attached to it. Third, because much of the work women do is unpaid, it tends not to get reported in official statistics. Even when women work for wages, especialy in the rural sector but also in urban piece-work employment, their wages are more often than not paid to the men. For the most current aggregate statistics see *Women in Pakistan: An Economic and Social Strategy*, A World Bank Country Study published in 1989.

[28] It needs to be recognised that this ideology not only serves as a means of enhancing one's sense of self, but also provides a distinction that may actually enable women to justify paid work by its designation as "respectable".

[29] Women's groups and human rights organisations in Pakistan have documented many cases in each of these categories.

[30] For more details see my article, "Women's Movement in Pakistan", *Pakistan Progressive*, Volume 5, No.1, 1983; Khawar Mumtaz and Fareeda Shahid, *Women of Pakistan* (London: Zed Books, 1987); Babar Ali, "Elitist View of Women's Struggle in Pakistan", *Economic and Political Weekly*, May 14, 1988; Shahnaz Rouse, "Class and Gender in Contemporary Pakistan: A Theoretical and Historical Exploration", mimeo, 1990.

Women and religious identities in India after Ayodhya

Gabriele Dietrich

This paper is an attempt to come to terms with the relationship women have with their religious identity in India after Ayodhya. If Ayodhya is a watershed it is due mainly to the fact that the destruction of the Babri Masjid on December 6, 1992, symbolised a breakdown of civil society and secular values in unprecedented ways. Things will never be the same again. However, the shift in identities, the rise of violence, the crisis of nationalism and the acceleration of destructive development policies which have precipitated the situation have been in the making for over a decade and more.

One question that urgently needs addressing is: Why did large numbers of women get co-opted into communal and fundamentalist formations? Why is it that the women's movement as an intervening force in communal carnage was hardly on the scene? Why did the few groups and movements which ventured out at that time get such little support?

In order to arrive at some understanding of these questions, I propose to reconstruct some of the debates on religion in the women's movement, and consider organisational changes within communal organisations and in other women's movements. Are we, in fact, confronted with a kind of communal fragmentation within the movement itself? If so, how do we deal with it? What is the connection between identity politics and changes in economic policies and in the overall development paradigm?

The historical debate on religion in the women's movement

Very briefly, the following positions can be discerned: till the mid-Eighties, religion was not a very hot topic in the women's movement in India. Enlightened opinion held that religious faith was a private affair, aided by generous doses of superstitious belief. Spirituality was a different matter altogether. Religion was also generally considered to be a patriarchal construct, oppressive of women, at best ignored, at worst, resisted and challenged.

Alongside was a school of thought which debated the "use of religion" for emancipatory purposes. This position worked on the assumption that

अहमदाबाद - सूरत - अयोध्या - बम्बई

religion is present among people anyway as a cultural force and that religious authority should not go uncontested. On the whole, proponents of this position were not too concerned with the question of faith but worked on the assumption that religion is instrumentalised anyway, either for reinforcing conservative controls or for progressive purposes. Opponents of this position pointed out that progressive forces will always be in a minority and, consequently, crediting religious sources will only strengthen religious authority.

It is important to understand that practising such a strategy yields different results in different religious contexts: whereas a progressive "use of religion" has been bravely tried out in various Islamic countries, the problem is that fundamentalism does not yield space for experimentation—historical criticism thus, is considered blasphemous.

In contrast to this, feminist Christian theologians placed themselves in the context of liberation theology. Though some of them speak in terms of a "usable past" their approach to religion is not simply instrumental. But they are constrained by the fact that western paradigms of feminist theology are not always easily applicable (eg., the whole debate on goddess religion makes little sense in a country teeming with goddesses and yet as bloomingly patriarchal as India), and on the whole, church women

have interacted rather little with the secular women's movement.

The different positions in the movement were hotly debated during the National Conference of the Autonomous Women's Movements in Bombay, in December 1985. Some groups took a militantly anti-religion stand, other people who were dealing with women's religiosity on a day-to-day basis were inclined to look upon it as a space in which the women found some respite and sustenance. There was an attempt to distinguish the oppressive aspects of religion and moves to communalise it, from its sustaining potential, and to work out a concept of "genuine religious reform" which could foster women's self-expression in religious terms.[1] This approach took serious note of the faith dimension in its own right and was distinct from the "progressive use of religion" school of thought.

This debate took place at a time when the communalisation of religion was already apparent: the Supreme Court judgement of 1985 in the Shah Bano case precipitated an identity crisis among Muslim fundamentalists and isolated Muslim reformers. Before the Bombay conference, a public meeting on the issue of a secular civil code took place, addressed among others by Indira Jaising, a lawyer of impeccable secular credentials, and Shehnaaz Sheikh, a Muslim divorcee who had herself challenged the Muslim law of divorce in the Supreme Court. The demand for a uniform civil code brought forward by them and by wide sections of the women's movement suddenly found itself in the company of majority communalist polemics; Shehnaaz Sheikh had to strenuously distinguish her position from "supporters" close to the Hindu fundamentalist Rashtriya Swayamsevak Sangh (RSS). The conference itself took place over

the women's movement could become a force against communalism.[2] At the time, the prevailing assumption was that women were mainly the victims of communal violence and not usually inclined to actively participate in it. An important point made was that women's organisations would be able to intervene against communalism only if they were able to build a viable mass base, especially

Let them create tiny Hindutvastan — the remaining subcontinent will be ours !

ISLAMIC BLOC

| Rajinder Puri: The Statesman

Christmas (which made it difficult for Christians to attend unless they were extraordinarily motivated) and at a time when the controversial Muslim Women's Bill was being heatedly debated in the country. Also within recall was the communal carnage that followed Indira Gandhi's assassination in 1984.

The debate focussed on whether

in urban slum areas. This is a task that most women's groups find hard to take up. By social convention, women's lives are fragmented between family chores, wage labour and movement activities. Their capacity to involve themselves in sustained organisational work is thus impaired both by social controls and physical constraints.

The emergence of majority communalism

Ever since the anti-Sikh massacre of 1984, the spectre of majority communalism has been haunting the women's movement. Recognising it as a formidable threat the Patna Conference of Autonomous Women's Movements passed a resolution in February 1988 explicitly condemning the attack on minorities.[3] The Conference also identified the role of the State in promoting communalism and fundamentalism and cited Shah Bano and the Deorala sati of Roop Kanwar as cases in point.

The Calicut Conference of Autonomous Women's Movements in 1990 held more extensive discussions on religion, fundamentalism and communalism. It became apparent that there exists a certain north-south divide in the religion and culture question: while fundamentalism and communalism are dominant problems in the north, women in the south are more overtly affected by caste conflicts. The Conference decided to observe March 8, 1991 as Anti-communal Day and to have a year-long campaign on the issue, although many of the women from the south felt frustrated that their perspective had been insufficiently incorporated.

The real extent of the spread of majority communalist culture was underlined by the National Conference on Women's Studies in Jadavpur University (Calcutta) in 1991. The Conference itself was devoted to the overall theme of communalism, fundamentalism and religious culture. A seminal contribution was made by Flavia Agnes, a lawyer from Bombay, who had earlier highlighted the issue of domestic violence and battered women with much personal involvement. Coming from a Catholic background but a self-professed non-believer herself, she made an attempt to reclaim certain Christian cultural symbols (eg. the cross as a symbol of suffering) or Christian feminist insights on theology as markers in her own history of suffering. She described how she had been put under pressure and suspicion of religious backwardness by her "secular" (Hindu) friends and even by her own daughters who wondered whether their mother had become senile in taking recourse to religious expressions. She contrasted this with the tacit assumptions of her "secular" Hindu friends that their displaying religious statues in their homes was entirely cultural and had nothing to do with religion. What she pleaded for was a truly pluralistic culture in which symbolic expressions drawn from all religions could be accessible to believers and non-believers alike.

Her presentation evoked very emotional responses from the audience and many women were confronted with their own unconscious majority communal assumptions for the first time. Another important contribution was made by Razia Patel, a Muslim woman from Ahmedabad with a "mixed" marriage. She recounted the incident of Muslim women being denied access to the cinema and their resistance, inviting threats of violence and denigration as traitors by fundamentalist men from her own community. Both presentations led to an extensive debate on religious identities, and to a recognition, virtually for the first time, that women in our country are divided not only before law but in our own midst by cultural practice. Intimations of this had come much earlier during the Trivandrum Conference of the Indian Association for Women's Studies in 1983, when there was great disagreement over whether the singing of *Vande Mataram* and the breaking of coconuts at the inaugural function were compatible with an avowed secular ethos. In Vishakapatnam in 1989, again at the IAWS Conference, there was considerable agitation over the imposition of Hindi with distinct religious overtones. However, the Calcutta Conference brought home the realisation that religious community is a social entity in its own right. There was strong agreement among the majority of participants that the richness of cultural diversity needs to be affirmed in view of the attempt by communal organisations and mass media to propagate universality and uniformity for a militarised form of Hinduism. The same Conference also saw some intensive discussion on caste and the relationship between Dalit and women's movements, though on the whole this aspect was under-represented.

While the realisation of internal cultural division within the women's movement was disconcerting, much more upsetting was the cooption of large numbers of women into the fold of communal organisations. Feminists were taken aback by hearing their own slogans being chanted by women of the saffron brigade: *Ham Bharat ki nari hain, phool nahin chingari hain.* (We are the women of Bharat, embers not flowers.) This came as something of a surprise since it was assumed that the patriarchal character and violent intervention of communal organisations would automatically marginalise women. There had also been a certain romanticism about the solidarity of women across religions. During a workshop of South Asian feminists in 1989, extensive discussions had taken place on this issue, during which it became obvious that communal identities were not only enforced by the State and by patriarchal men but that women had also voluntarily exercised the communal option.[4]

The realisation that women are also in the forefront in promoting communal violence is unavoidable after Ayodhya and its aftermath. It is not limited to the active incitement of Uma Bharati and Sadhvi Rithambara in the

मंदिर भी लेलो, मस्जिद भी लेलो
मगर तुम हमारे धर्म से न खेलो

Jagori , New Delhi

demolition of the mosque; much worse was women's role in the ensuing riots when they tore off other women's clothes and facilitated rape.

Some of this has to do with ideological constructs and some with concerted organisational effort on the part of communal and fundamentalist groups to draw women in. While women of the "minorities" are bulldozed and streamlined into communal conformity in response to attacks from the outside, majority communal adjustments are of a more complex nature. Partly, of course, the ideology of the majority over the past few years has "done a Sri Lanka", i.e., it has fanned anxieties of Hinduism being in danger from pan-Islamic forces all over the world, just as the Sinhala majority has anticipated a threat from the millions of Tamils just across the Palk Strait. This mechanism is analogous to the disciplining appeal to Muslim women that "Islam is in danger" (and, therefore, reforms are out!). Such adjustments work fairly well, though the actual patriarchal content of communal organisations also works against the involvement of women.[5]

The subtle appeal is both ideological and organisational and both aspects are worked out in complementarity. Tanika Sarkar, who has done pioneering work in analysing this phenomenon, has described how communal organisations like the RSS and VHP (Vishwa Hindu Parishad)

have put in enormous effort to rope in women and youngsters *without questioning patriarchal family ideology*.[6] Indeed, the wider organisation is perceived to be an extension of the family and thus, women's involvement is acceptable. In this way, women not only acquire militancy without questioning traditional roles, they even acquire skills in yoga and the martial arts which are useful for self-defence in any situation. Women so involved need not fear criticism or antagonism; no one chastises them for their public activities, nor are they seen to be undermining the family. At the same time they gain status, power, ability and skills. This is backed by ideological constructs which project equality with a difference (women and men are equal but not the same) and the concept of "complementarity". Ratna Kapur and Brenda Cossmann have sensitively analysed these constructs and shown that they are not all that easy to dismantle, for the simple reason that a more consistently feminist approach requires the organisation of support systems which, in real life, are not easily available.[7]

These new configurations have revealed that women are not only ideologically divided, experiencing fundamental organisational problems, but that even the issue of violence is by no means a unifying factor among women any more. This was eloquently put forward by Flavia Agnes during the Mysore IAWS Conference in May 1993. She had worked with an organisation after the Bombay riots of early 1993, and had encountered the most intricate difficulties in keeping violence under control. Rape was no longer simply a women's issue, it had become communal. Allies and adversaries changed according to the issues and women were deeply divided among themselves. This we had been forced to acknowledge earlier in discussions with Dalit women: violence is caste and class specific. Upper caste women face more domestic violence but the vast majority of rural rapes are perpetuated publicly on Dalit women. It now became necessary to acknowledge that the brunt of communal violence is borne by minority women (Sikhs in 1984, Muslims after Ayodhya) and that there has been an attempt by Hindutvadis to rope in Dalits and Adivasis in the assault on Muslims. Such attempts may appear attractive not only as a short-cut to rehabilitation for Dalit and Adivasi men but even for women who may see this as a means to resolve their own problem of caste violence. Tanika Sarkar has drawn our attention to the current focus of Hindu communal organisations on Dalit and Adivasi women.[8]

Within the women's movement, however, we have not done our homework regarding the problems of Dalit women and this may be one chief reason why our resistance to communalism has remained rather toothless.[9] It is important to own the experiences of the women in Ambedkar's movement as the common history of women's struggles.

The emergence of majority communalism has also made the struggle for a common civil code extremely difficult. Even the most outspoken Muslim reformers today feel that the Muslim family law cannot be done away with. Some have pointed out that uniformity presupposes a monolithic view of the nation state and does not necessarily serve the cause of social justice or women's rights.[10]

Christians too have been knocking around with the reform of their divorce law and women's right to property. After Mary Roy's spectacular legal victory in the Supreme Court on the Travancore Christian Succession Act* the issue today is being bitterly contested and there are attempts afoot to invalidate the retrospective effect of the Supreme Court judgement. The Christian divorce law is one of the worst possible for women and despite years of struggle by organisations like the Joint Women's Programme, little progress has been made.

The link between cultural identities and organic life: women as vestiges of culture

If one thing has become clear over the past few years, it is the fact that caste

*See Mary Roy's Testimony in this journal for details.

and religious community are much stronger in women's lives than gender, at least in situations of communal strife.[11] While patriarchal violence persists as crippling and, at times, life-threatening in daily life, the "external" threat of communal violence becomes overwhelming in times of conflict. Thus, the present climate of heightened communal tension unavoidably strengthens patriarchal controls within the community. At the same time, the process of women embodying the vestiges of culture has its own internal logic of women's empowerment with patriarchal approval.

Women's link with caste and community underlines and is made via, the family. One chief problem seems to be that the production of life itself has been taking place in patriarchal institutions. This not only pertains to producing children but has to do with the transmission of culture itself. This takes place not only at the intellectual and doctrinal levels, but through the details of daily organisation — food habits, pollution taboos, who we eat and sleep with, how we dress, body language, and so on. As women are crucial in the organisation of the home and the socialisation of children, cultural control over them is fundamental to the continuity, not only of the race, but of tradition and communal identity itself. The production of life and cultural controls are thus intrinsically related. Engels' view that inheritance of property was the key issue, is only one aspect of the problem; feminists in the meantime have discovered the constitutive function of violence in establishing control. Without this control men's very access to children and the continuity of life is imperilled. Beyond the control over sexuality, fertility and 'labour, however, men's control over culture by constructing women as its vestiges, also needs critical attention.

If we in the women's movement have found it difficult to see these connections more sharply, it is probably due to our failure to come to terms with the concept of the family: we have attacked it as the fountainhead of patriarchal power without adequately understanding that women have not just been passive victims of violence but a crucial lifeline, not only for the continuity of life itself but also as a key to tradition and cultural identity. The south Indian concept of *karpu* (chastity) is founded on the very real anxiety in men that if women's sexuality is not controlled, actual identities will change in unimaginable ways.

Ideology of motherhood

One powerful fix that codifies the ambiguity of women as powerful, yet under control, is the symbol of motherhood, which in many way is crosscultural. Of course, there are great variations in the extent of patriarchal control; nor is motherhood, strictly speaking, a religious ideology, it can occur in the secular realm as well.[12]

The link between motherhood-ideology and nationalism came into sharp focus during the Hindu renaissance in Bengal. As Jasodhara Bagchi put it: "Bengali mothers proverbially stood for unstinting affection, manifested in an undying spirit of self-sacrifice for the family. The social reform era, when there was vigorous protest against the overt oppression of women (child marriage, perpetual widowhood for caste Hindu women, widow-burning) considered motherhood in a very positive light... Mothers were justified by the greatness of their sons".[13] Motherhood was also used by some nationalists to establish ideological control over women, to keep them out of education and professions, to reduce them to their reproductive roles. At the same time they were glorified for their ability to sacrifice, and conceptualised as mothers of the nation; as such, the benevolent powers of the goddess were ascribed to them.

A revival of the ideology of motherhood in a secular garb —albeit with religious overtones—can be observed in the ideology of the Sangh Parivar. Mother India is projected as being in danger of being raped and dismembered. The rapist is, of course, the Muslim, and the rape of women and of the nation are collapsed into one. Against this, a militant Hinduism is mobilised which also uses the metaphor of the family to express hegemony: Vasudeva Kuttumbkam—the world is one family.[14]

Family-caste-community-nation

Where does all this leave us? Events have forced us to recognize that our assumption that the very existence of patriarchy in the family and other institutions is a uniting factor for women, holds true only in times of relative peace. Communal and caste organisation facilitates an empowerment of sorts with the support of the patriarchal family. The ideology of motherhood is an important catalysing factor in this process of cooption and even organisationally, the family appears to be an important recruitment area for women's political activism — in contrast to the feminist option where activism entails distancing from the patriarchal family.

One crucial question that any movement for transformation faces is how it relates to the organic elements of social organisation, i.e., family, caste and community. Movements like the feminist one have for a long time assumed that caste, class and community cannot divide us. At the same time, we have not fully explored the supportive qualities of the family and options for living in family-like units of support, which are not patriarchal in character. Individualism as it has developed in western countries is not feasible in a poverty-stricken society where economic and cultural survival

धार्मिक कट्टरपंथी राज्य में औरतों का भविष्य
ख़ामोशी दमन बर्दन

Women's future under fundamentalism:
silence suppression oppression

are often attained through clusters of support.

Along with this, the issue of genuine religious reform is as burning as ever. It is only recently that the debate on communalism has acknowledged the question of faith in its own right.[15] Rustom Bharucha has suggested that faith itself is a resource for communal harmony (his words in God's ear, one might wish) but this cannot be a matter for theoretical discussion only. As women's movements have moved from "women's issues proper" to survival issues like public distribution, alternative agriculture and resource control, housing and basic amenities, labour in the nonformal sector, and so on, they have found that organisational work must take place in cooperation with "mixed" organisations like unions in the informal sector, ecological movements and cultural movements. It is in such organisational work that questions of identity, faith, religious reform, counter-culture and alternative family structures need to be raised and resolved.

Culture, religion and development

Any assessment of trends would be incomplete without connecting the issue of identity, culture and religion to the impact of recent development policies. It is not coincidental that the breakdown of Nehruvian secularism in post-Independence India has been simultaneous with the dismantling of "socialist" paraphernalia in the economic realm. There is a close connection between the New Economic Policy (NEP) and the rise of communalism. This connection is evident even superficially, as it is a worldwide trend. In all the former socialist countries, identity politics and communal strife have flared up, often taking the form of civil war. This has partly to do with greater competition as a result of the more aggressive penetration of world capitalism, and partly a reaction to the uniformity of technocratic, individualistic western consumer culture. This last, in the face of an ecological resource crisis is material evidence for the non-viability of growth-oriented development which is being projected as the only option.

One will have to add that what is at stake today is people's very right to life and livelihood, in jeopardy through privatisation and displacement. But resistance is growing. Movements like Narmada Bachao Andolan are today trying to coordinate all sorts of campaigns against World Bank projects in the country. The National Alliance of People's Movements called for concerted protest against the Dunkel Draft on Republic Day,1994. It appeals to all secular and egalitarian mass organisations to:

— oppose the politics of religion which is dividing our people;

— oppose New Economic Policy which, through measures like Dunkel and the entry of multinationals, is fostering consumerism, displacement and corruption in the guise of liberation;

— uphold the rights of the common people (tribals, farmers and workers) to have a say in the consumption of national resources like water, forest and land.

Ultimately it will certainly dawn on people that survival issues cannot be solved through communal organisations and that the communalisation of politics works not only against the "other" but against the right to life and livelihood in general.

The real onslaught of the NEP today is against the cohesiveness of the social structure. Privatisation enhances competition and insecurity; demarcation of caste and community gets sharper in this situation and can erupt in conflict at any time. Nevertheless, people try to gather strength and fight back unitedly. Dalit and anti-Brahmin forces are an important factor in this context but cannot come up with alternatives on their own. Alliances are crucial but difficult to build. Women of the weaker sections are particularly hard hit by rising prices, the dismantling of the public distribution system, disinvestment in social services, and overcrowding of the informal sector due to drastic cutbacks in the organised sector.[16] But women are organising. Having been exposed to the culture of workers in the informal sector over the years, I am deeply convinced that many of these people, while in no way preoccupied with religion, have a religious faith which enhances their humanitarian concern and is not, in itself, communal.

Jeremy Seabrook in a recent book has pointed out how immensely destructive development processes in this century have been.[17] People do not want this kind of change. They want a revolution as it was conceptualised by the Left. They want to resist by constructing places of refuge, stability, tranquility and peace where people's life will be protected in a neighbourhood which safeguards self-reliance and kinship, the protection of life and livelihood. As feminists, we have had to battle against the fetters attached to such tranquility. We also know that the transformation required is indeed formidable. The communalists, on the other hand, lure people with a false sense of belonging which will create enormous destruction. Popular culture is prepared to resist this destruction, but how we draw on it to build units of living which will give shelter without being a prison to women, dalits and other oppressed sections, is as yet an unresolved task.

The question which we will have to answer over the next few years is not only how we defend this popular religious and secular culture against the onslaught of mass media and communal forces, but how we make our different cultures accessible to each other so that we can be sustained in our struggles for control over basic resources, as well as in our search for a dignified life in which respect for all will be safeguarded.

Notes

[1] See my article, "Women's Movement and Religion: Reflections on the Women's Movement in India", *Religion, Ecology, Development* (Horizon India Books, New Delhi 1992,) pp. 13-34.

[2] See my article, "Can the Women's Movement be a Force Against Communalism? in *Women's Movement in India: Conceptual and Religious Reflections* (Breakthrough Publications, Bangalore 1989) pp. 187-201

[3] *Women and Struggle*, A Report of the Nari Mukti Sangharsh Sammelan, Patna 1988 (ed. Gail Omvedt, Chetna Gala, Govind Kelkar, Kali for Women, New Delhi, 1988).

[4] See Amrita Chhachhi: "Identity Politics" in this journal.

[5] See e.g. Veena Poonacha, "Hindutva's Hidden Agenda: Why Women Fear Religious Fundamentalism", *Economic & Political Weekly*, March 13, 1992.

[6] See e.g. Tanika Sarkar: "The Woman as Communal Subject: Rashtra Sevika Samiti and Ram Janmabhoomi Movement", *EPW* Aug.31,1991.

See also her article: "The Sangh Parivar's Strategy of Forming a Women's Wing" with its accent on values that do not question patriarchy, *Pioneer*, Dec.23, 1992.

[7] Quoted in Ratna Kapur & Brenda Cossman: "Communalising Gender/Engendering Community: Women, Legal Discourse and Saffron Agenda" in *EPW* April 24, 1993.

[8] Tanika Sarkar, op.cit.

[9] For a deeper analysis of this problem see my article "Dalit Movements and Women's Movements" in *Reflections on the Women's Movement in India* .

[10] See e.g. Iqbal A. Ansari, "Muslim Women's Rights: Goals and Strategy of Reform" in *EPW* April 27, 1991.

[11] See e.g. the interesting survey by Bhavna Mehta and Trupti Shah: "Gender and Communal Riots" in *EPW* No.21, 1992.

[12] The issue of Review of Women's Studies in EPW on Ideology of Motherhood (Oct. 20-27, 1990) is highly instructive in this context.

[13] Jasodhara Bagchi, "Representing Nationalism: Ideology of Motherhood in Colonial Bengal" in *EPW* Oct. 20-27, 1990.

[14] See e.g. Sudhir Kakar's analysis of Sadhvi Ritambara's speech in *The Telegraph* reproduced in *Divided We Stand as Ayodhya Sets the Agenda*, Delhi Forum, Dec. 1993, Part VI.

[15] Rustom Barucha, *The Question of Faith*, (Orient Longman 1993).

[16] Gabriele Dietrich, "Effects of IMF/WB Policies on Women in India", Vikalp-Alternatives Vol.II, 2/3, 1993, pp. 8-11.

[17] Jeremy Seabrook, *Victims of Development: Resistance and Alternatives* (London: Verso, 1993).

Poster: Sheba Chhachhi. Produced by ASR, Lahore.

Islam, feminism, and the women's movement in Pakistan: 1981-91

Fauzia Gardezi

It can be said that the current women's movement in Pakistan began with the formation of the Women's Action Forum (WAF) in 1981.[1] This organisation began as an urgent effort to unite women and women's organisations to combat the attack on women launched by General Zia-ul Haq's martial law government. No doubt feminist struggle in Pakistan pre-dates the formation of WAF, but the regular incidence of women taking collective action specifically against their oppression as women, and the level of awareness created of the need for change in this regard, was new to this period.

More than ten years later, WAF itself is still active and women's awareness continues to grow. In addition, Pakistani women are still fighting State action against them. The threat posed to women by the Shariat Bill passed in May 1991 and plans for a separate women's university, both legacies of the Zia period, are among the issues confronting the Pakistani women's movement today.[2]

The focus in this discussion is not on the measures taken by Zia's government, or the specific issues women were fighting against during this period;[3] rather, it will take a broader look at some of the more theoretical problems and debates that have emerged within the movement during the last few years.

Feminism from within Islam

The need to develop frameworks to guide action and provide direction to the movement became apparent after a period of what was often, of necessity, hastily-planned, reactive responses to issues set by the martial law government.[4] Two of the main problems encountered by the women's movement in Pakistan have been *(i)* trying to work within an Islamic framework; and *(ii)* insufficient incorporation of feminism in the movement.

The major recent debate within WAF has been whether or not a struggle against patriarchy should be waged from within the framework of Islam. In part, the need to work within Islam arose from the fact that the anti-women legislation and actions taken by Zia's government were declared to be part of a programme of Islamisation. Various Islamic laws were proposed or enacted such as the Hadood Ordinances, the Law of Evidence and the law on Qisas and

The Hadood Ordinance deals with the offences of prohibition (consumption of drugs and alcohol), *zina* (rape, adultery, fornication), theft and *qazf* (perjury). It is with regard to *zina* that the Hadood Ordinance has been most controversial.

Prior to 1979, adultery and fornication were not crimes against the State. Under the Hadood Ordinance both are now serious offences liable for the heaviest of punishment — death, and that too, by stoning.

Zina is defined as wilful sex between two adults who are not validly married to each other. Where sex takes place against the will or consent of a person (either man or woman), or by use of force, or where one person is falsely led to believe that his/her partner is validly married to him/her, it is defined as *zina-bil-jabr*.

Both types of *zina* are liable to the *hadd* punishment (stoning to death in public) if either a confession is obtained, or if the actual act of penetration is witnessed by *four adult, pious, and forthright males*. Failing this the lighter punishment of *tazir* (rigorous imprisonment and whipping) applies. *Tazir* is given when, despite there being no witnesses or confession, the court is convinced that *zina* or *zina-bil-jabr* took place.

Diyat.* These laws made it difficult to prove the crime of rape, put rape victims at risk of being charged with adultery, and reduced the worth of a woman, and her testimony in some cases, to half that of a man. Islam was also used to justify various government directives on women's dress, a plan to create a separate women's university, and an unwritten ban on women's participation in spectator sports.

Thus, it was felt that there was a need to show that opposition to these laws and measures was not necessarily opposition to Islam; yet the paradox soon grew into a debate on the wisdom of the strategic use of Islam. One view is presented by Shahnaz Rouse who argues that what is needed is "a movement that poses resolution of its problems in opposition to Islamic discourse. The point is not to reject Islam, but to clearly state that the issue of women's rights is a secular issue of human rights."[5] On the other hand, Mumtaz and Shaheed argue that Islam is part of Pakistan's culture; in order not to be perceived as alien, there is a need to operate within Pakistani culture and, therefore, within Islam.[6] In addition, they state that, while upper and upper-middle class women may prefer a secular women's movement, a discussion of women's rights within Islam is needed to appeal to lower-middle class and working class women.[7]

* See Shahla Zia's essay in this journal for details.

The Women's Action Forum, particularly the Lahore chapter, has often subscribed to the latter position in the last ten years, but there are real problems with this approach. While working within Islam may win the support of some women, it does not mean that an alternative mobilisation around a discourse based on a strong critique of patriarchal social relations and social structures, cannot take place. More importantly, working within the Islamic discourse in many ways threatens the struggle against women's oppression, all round.

At the very outset, it makes over power to Islamic fundamentalists, the very ones who have endorsed women's oppression and subordination. The framing of a discourse in terms of Islam is stated by the Islamic right-wing themselves to be their greatest source of power. For example, one member of the Jamaat-e-Islami, when asked about their success given their poor showing in the elections, responded that they "had changed the way people spoke: people (were) now forced to speak in Islamic terms".[8] Some in the women's movement believe that there is a need to counter fundamentalist interpretations of Islam with more progressive ones,[9] but the trouble is that there are innumerable interpretations among the "experts" themselves; the women's movement will simply be adding its voice to the many others, and a victory for progressive forces is not likely on the fundamentalists' own terrain. As Shahnaz Rouse says, this will contribute to "thwarting a return to democratic norms and secular discussion".[10] Should the women's movement actually be instrumental in this, it might well end up defeating itself.

There is also the danger that focusing too much on Islam and what it says about women will detract from attempts to address women's real problems. One active WAF member whom I interviewed expressed the concern that Islam was not an important issue in the minds of the majority of poor women, and that the entire debate over whether to take a secular or an Islamic approach was sidetracking the struggle.[11] Mumtaz and Shaheed describe how the Lahore chapter of WAF has used Islam to appeal to women, yet it has not always taken up the problems of their everyday existence. In one instance WAF failed to help a group of women who lost their jobs because of their involvement in union activities.[12] Through such actions and the general focus on the centrality of Islam, WAF risks giving people more religion while neglecting their material problems, a tendency which runs counter to feminism and to progress.

Finally, the view that one must work within Islam because it is part of the culture of Pakistan, in itself subordinates women and undermines the feminist struggle through some of its implications. Patriarchy, too, is part of the culture — one cannot challenge patriarchal relations while conforming to its dictates. This argument is tantamount to saying that one cannot fight for women's rights because the culture does not permit it; and while it suggests that those who do not work within Islam will be perceived as alien, one would not want to lend credence to the oft-expressed view that they are in fact, so.

One must also look into the whole question of legitimation. Do those who want to restrict women's rights in the name of Islam derive their power from the support of the people? Have the anti-women laws enacted in the name of Islam been passed by governments with popular mandates? The answers are clearly related to the issue of whether or not the women's movement needs to give primacy to challenging the Islamic character of these laws and other attacks on women. WAF has had some success in mobilising some women, from a particular class or income group, by pointing out how the laws are un-Islamic;[13] the point here is not to deny this, but to suggest that an alternative discourse may also mobilise large numbers of women, from this class and others, without the inherent dangers already discussed.

The argument that an appeal to Pakistani cultural norms and Islam is of central importance in gaining people's support, suggests that a woman's perception of the world and her behaviour will be influenced more by ideal factors than her own concrete life experiences, and an appeal based on these. One cannot, of course, ignore the role of hegemonic discourses in influencing people's outlook and behaviour. But in a country in which the majority of people, particularly women, are illiterate, have no exposure to State-controlled media, and only intermittently to fundamentalist propaganda, it would be difficult to recruit them to the world-view of the ruling group. While Islam may be an important part of many people's lives, it is not the same as the Islam of the fundamentalists. Indeed, if electoral politics are any indication, repressive, fundamentalist Islam as projected by the extreme right wing, has been rejected each time.

Bringing feminism into the movement

While the question of working within Islam may have been the main source of disagreement within WAF during the last ten years, women disagreed as well around the issue of feminism and the movement. By and large the Pakistani women's movement avoids using this term;[14] at times, it is even presented as being opposed to feminism, which is seen to be "western" and "alien".

Apart from questioning the motives of some of those who attack feminism, there is also a misconception of what feminism actually is. There may well be a narrow strain within feminism which views the struggle as simply one of achieving equality with men, while not calling for any broader restructuring of society. But, increasingly, there is a realisation that feminism cannot be reduced solely to a concern with gender inequality, because this ignores the inequalities that exist among men. Again, women have different experiences based on characteristics other than gender; to struggle around gender alone is to downgrade this diversity and generalise the experiences of women. Feminism is and must be every woman's movement and the only way it can achieve this is to bring every woman's experiences into its fold.

This is not to say that what women experience specifically, based on their gender, is a lesser form of oppression than, for example, that based on class. Mumtaz and Shaheed rightly point out that gender-based oppression for upper class women in Pakistan is one of the few types of oppression they experience, while for other women it is one of many.[15] But this does not diminish the importance of gender-related experiences for poorer women, nor does it mean that "the women's issue does not have the same immediacy for working class women as it does for upper class women".[16] It must be understood that gender issues include violence against women, women's economic dependency, and male control over women's lives. These are not issues that only more privileged women can afford to address; they are bread and butter issues — often, life-and-death issues. Therefore, one must not minimise the impact that they have on the lives of poor or working class women, or subordinate them to other issues when talking of women in oppressed classes. A gender-based struggle cannot be waged alone, but it must also not be compromised.

The lack of a clear feminist framework has led to difficulties in conceptualising problems facing women in Pakistan, and uncertainty within WAF about which issues to support. The decision by WAF in Lahore not to support trade union women in a conflict with their employer was informed by a very narrow, and ultimately untenable, definition of feminism. Even with this definition, the issue should have been supported because of its implications for women's economic independence, and their inroads into the male-dominated formal labour force and labour movement. It may be that the reason these women were not supported has more to do with the class composition of WAF[17] and its failure to employ class and feminist analyses, than with feminism itself.

Mumtaz and Shaheed suggest that because of instances such as this, WAF should focus on "women's rights" rather than "feminism". The problem is that the former does not provide the necessary tools for generating fundamental social change, for which the concepts and analyses of feminism cannot be dispensed with. Many of WAF's disagreements can be seen as arising from the lack of a coherent and consistent theoretical base, leaving the organisation prey to the inclinations of its individual members.

A closer identification with feminism is also desirable in order to avoid problems, encountered by WAF in the past, of giving in to some aspects of patriarchal culture in order to gain support. Mumtaz and Shaheed state that : "[WAF's] desire to raise consciousness among the widest sections of society and elicit their tacit, if not overt, support meant that in making concessions to Pakistani culture it compromised a purely feminist line."[18] As a result, smoking in public for example, was avoided by members and there was a concern that WAF's protest against the exclusion of women from spectator sports cost them supporters.[19] However, while these activities may be an affront to Pakistani patriarchal culture, and may not be issues directly affecting the greater number of Pakistani women, there *are* female athletes in Pakistan and women who want to smoke. The question is whether WAF is a feminist organisation or whether it joins the ranks of those who proscribe women's behaviour because they are women. It matters little that one's position is based on the belief that such issues are, indeed, wrong, or on the fact that other people think that they are wrong; the end result is the same. By not wanting to alienate anybody, there is the risk of backing away from a challenge to patriarchal culture, and alienating feminists themselves.

Conclusion

During the last ten years, Pakistani women have shown that they will not submit to State attempts to remove them from the public sphere and diminish their legal rights. While showing strength in this regard, certain tendencies within the women's movement have the potential to weaken it considerably. A transformation of the movement to a radical, secular, feminist one faces many difficulties. One problem is that, over time in Pakistan, the ability to come out openly in favour of secularism in mainstream political discourse has been lost. Women must fight this trend. Obviously, a secular state is no guarantee of women's rights, but the inability to talk of the separation of Islam from the State, laws, educational systems, media, and other institutions has blunted the struggle against Islamisation, somewhat. The passing of the Shariat Bill in 1991 has only served to underline this.

The women's movement and WAF are not alone in their fight against the Shariat Bill. The move toward re-establishing a secular, democratic politics in Pakistan is an endeavour concerning many groups. Thus, the women's movement could derive strength by forging links with other groups fighting for political and social change. Some links have already been made, particularly by the Karachi chapter of WAF.[20] However, there is always the problem of women's concerns being subordinated to other issues when such links are made. The extent to which groups with a common agenda come together probably depends not so much on WAF and the women's movement as on whether or not the left in Pakistan is willing to make feminism part of its struggle.

Accompanying an attempt to include a secular ideology in the women's movement should be a stronger focus on the material problems of everyday existence faced by women in Pakistan. A possible starting point would be further research on the actual status of women, largely unknown for the majority of women in Pakistan. The small amount of information available is often inaccurate leading, for example, to ridiculously low official estimates of the number of women who are economically active. In addition, the women's movement may find it useful to look at feminist movements in other countries, how they have sought support, and how they have responded to attacks on feminism. It is scarcely more socially acceptable to call oneself a feminist in most other countries, including those in the west. Similarly, the attempt to use culture, or some aspect of it, to subvert the cause of feminism is not unique to Pakistan.

Finally, analysing the history of women's movements can assist in building strong feminist movements in Pakistan and elsewhere. There is a need to look at the theoretical and practical implications of past activities and work towards uilding frameworks for understanding women's oppression. It is through such an endeavour that one can understand the task of the feminist movement, and the strategies that it should employ in the future.

Notes

This article has been adapted from an earlier version which appeared in *Viewpoint* (Lahore, August 15, 1991.)

[1] Khawar Mumtaz and Farida Shaheed, *Women of Pakistan: Two Steps Forward, One Step Back?* (London: Zed Books, 1987), p.123.

[2] Trouble for women can be foreseen in two clauses of the Bill: it states that the government will take measures to combat obscenity, a term which has in the past been equated with women themselves (see *ibid.*, pp.81-3); second, a clause requiring citizens to regulate their lives according to the Shariat has the potential to curtail the rights of women, as pointed out by Asma Jahangir, "On the Offensive", *Herald*, Vol.22, No.5, May 1991, pp.29-30. In addition, any law giving greater power to the Islamic clergy is a threat to women and the few rights they have obtained in Pakistan.

[3] In addition to Mumtaz and Shaheed, *op.cit.*, see Shahnaz Rouse, "Women's Movement in Pakistan : State, Class, Gender", *South Asia Bulletin*, Vol. VI, No.1, Spring, 1986, pp. 30-7, and Nighat Said Khan, "Women in Pakistan: A New Era?" (Lahore: ASR, 1988).

[4] See Mumtaz and Shaheed, *op.cit.*, p.148. They address the issue of how WAF is now encountering difficulty in moving from being a reactive organisation to one which takes the initiative in setting its own agenda.

[5] Rouse, *op. cit.*, p.36.

6   Mumtaz and Shaheed, *op. cit.*, p.131.

7   *Ibid.*, pp. 131-32.

8   Emma Duncan, *Breaking the Curfew: A Political Journey Through Pakistan* (London: Arrow Books, 1989), p.231.

9   Mumtaz and Shaheed, *op. cit.*, p.156.

10   Rouse, *op. cit..* p.36.

11   The following was stated by a WAF working committee member in Islamabad during an interview in May 1991: "Our line has been that WAF should not be wasting time with (secular versus Islamic) issues. The real issues are development and why women have to slog it out more than men. That is a different line where one is trying to veer WAF . . . I don't agree with the idea that women will join you in terms of Islam. More people will join you if you talk about violence, issues of survival. Islam is not on their minds."

12   Mumtaz and Shaheed, *op. cit.*, p.150.

13   These women were from the lower-middle and working classes in urban areas; *ibid.*, p.132, 142n. The majority of support for right-wing Islamic parties tends to come from the new urban middle class. It would be interesting to investigate whether these two facts are related.

14   The author was told, for example, by a WAF working committee member in Islamabad that most members in that chapter would not call themselves feminists.

15   Mumtaz and Shaheed, *op. cit.*, p.151.

16   *Ibid.*

17   They are largely from upper-middle or upper class backgrounds.

18   Mumtaz and Shaheed, op. cit., p.131.

19   *Ibid.*, pp. 131-2.

20   *Ibid.*, p.126.

Women, religion and law

Indira Jaising

Prepared at a South Asian Women and Development Workshop in Bangladesh, organised by FAO FFHC/AD (New Delhi), SAWF (Colombo) and Nari Pokho (Dhaka). Produced by ASR (Lahore).

With every passing year, the involvement of the State with religion makes a mockery of its secular pretensions. For women this has meant State-supported oppression by religious obscurantists of all hues. Since women have rarely been a part of organised religious leadership anywhere, they have little experience of challenging religious oppression; but until religion itself is challenged, the fate of women's equality will be left not to the gods, but to fundamentalist religious authorities. A few examples from recent memory will serve to illustrate the point.

In 1986, Shahida Parveen's husband divorced her; she was childless and he wanted a new wife. As a divorced woman in Pakistan, Shahida was subject to ridicule and attack and hence, three months later, she married her cousin. On November 7, 1987, a judge ruled that her divorce papers were invalid and that she was therefore guilty of adultery. Under the law of Islam she was punished to death by stoning. Shahida now awaits her sentence in a jail in Pakistan, a victim not of misdeed or misfortune, but of religious fundamentalism.

Impact of fundamentalism

In country after country throughout the world, the revival of religious fundamentalism has been accompanied by the increasing oppression of women. In the west, Christian fundamentalists preach against abortion and argue that women should return to their "rightful" place in the home. In Iran, women helped to overthrow the Shah, but with Ayatollah Khomeini's accession to power, all women's rights were abolished through legislation. Among other things, he abolished day-care and reintroduced the compulsory chador which had been banned since 1936. In Kuwait, religious authorities recently decreed that Muslim women be denied the right to vote or run for Parliament, stating, "The nature of the electoral process befits men who are endowed with ability and expertise. It is not possible that women recommend or nominate other women or men for public posts. Islam does not permit women to forfeit their basic commitment — bearing and rearing children."

Religion within the Indian Constitution

India today presents a picture of excessive government entanglement with religion. Whether it is the screening of the *Ramayana* and *Mahabharata* on Doordarshan, or the publication of religious texts at reduced prices, the active support to religion is all-pervasive. The recent controversy in Maharashtra over the proscribing of *Riddles of Hinduism* by Dr. B.R. Ambedkar is another instance of government regulation of educational material. Not only has the government in this case published a book on religion at its own cost, it has also assumed the role of censor and the right to decide what part or portion of critical writing on religion should be published.

Is such an involvement with religion by the State constitutionally permissible? Is it any answer to say that all religious communities are guaranteed their "personal" laws, hence no religious group is being discriminated against? Could the government, for example, argue that while the *Ramayana* is being serialised on Doordarshan, religious texts of other communities are also being serialised and therefore the religious freedom of all communities is assured? Can the State justify its failure to reform family law on the ground that to do so would be to violate the constitutional guarantee of freedom of religion?

This assumption of the role of censor and arbiter, interpreter and custodian of religion is a logical consequence of the entry of the State into the realm of religion. To accept such an argument would be to horribly misunderstand the meaning of the right to freedom of religion guaranteed by Article 25.

In fact, acceptance of such an argument can lead to fanning the flames of fundamentalism. The freedom of religion then ends up being a guarantee of the right to be communal. The continued enforcement of religious laws in matters pertaining to the family is tantamount to supporting communal rather than secular values by the State. Relegating the family to the realm of private as opposed to pulic law and linking it up with religion, ensures a hands-off policy by the State to women's issues and effectively consigns them to mullahs and pandits.

Article 25 perverted

Article 25 says that subject to public order, morality and health, and suject to the other fundamental guarantees (right to equality, the right not be discriminated against on grounds of sex, race or religion) all persons are equally entitled to freedom of conscience and the right to freely profess, propagate and practice religion. Article 25 makes it clear that the State can make laws regulating and restricting any economic, financial, political, or other secular practice which may be associated with religion. The State can also enact laws for social reform and welfare. Article 26, which is an aspect of Article 25, guarantees to every religious denomination, the right to establish, maintain and administer institutions of religious or charitable nature. Article 27, a much ignored provision, is in essence a "non-establishment of religion" clause. No discussion of Article 25 can be complete without an understanding of Article 27. Whereas Article 25 guarantees freedom of religion to the individual, Article 27 *prevents the State from entanglement with it*. Without Article 27, the right under Article 25 can end up guaranteeing the right to the State to

support communalism.

We argue that the guarantee under Article 25 is patently unconstitutional. First, the enforcement of religious laws results in direct violations of the fundamental right to equality for women and discriminates against them on grounds of religion alone. Second, by enforcing religious laws, the State is in fact "establishing religion". What is not clearly understood is that the guarantee of freedom of religion makes no sense without a corresponding injunction against the State preventing it from establishing religion. State entanglement with religion in any form is antithetical to the negative injunction preventing the establishment of religion, an injunction implicit in the Constitution, running right through the Preamble, the Fundamental Rights and the Directive Principles of State Policy. Thus, while the citizen is guaranteed the right to freedom of conscience, belief and religion, the State is correspondingly debarred from implicating itself in any religious matters or in establishing it.

Core test incorrect

The current judicial analysis of the scope of the guaranteed right to freedom of religion, its meaning, content and limitations, is entirely wrong. While deciding whether a particular law violates freedom of religion, judges have got hopelessly entangled in finding out whether the law interferes with the "essential core" or practice of the religion. If it does, it is held to be bad, if it does not it passes the test and is held to be valid. This test for determining the constitutional validity of a law alleged to violate freedom of religion is quite incorrect and leads to dangerous conclusions, namely, that if a law interferes with the essential core of religion, it is unconstitutional regardless of the fact that it seeks to achieve some form of secular regulation. For example, if a law is enacted abolishing polygamy, or unilateral divorce among Muslims, or conferring equal rights of inheritance for men and women, and it is found that these practices form part of the "essential core" of religion, can it be argued that the law abolishing them is unconstitutional and violative of Article 25? What about the right to equality for women? Articles 14 & 15 would have to be rewritten to mean that subject to the freedom to practice religion, women shall have both the right to equality *and the right not to be discriminated against.*

The courts' answers to the question of what is or isn't a core practice of religion have yielded inconsistent determinations. Constitutionally, the courts' focus should be on the necessity of the State law or regulation in question, rather than on whether or not it alters the "essential core" of a religion. The true test of judging whether a particular State law violates Article 25 would be to pose the question - is there a compelling State interest in making the law? Article 25 permits the State, in unambiguous terms, to make laws for social reform, public order and so on. In any given case, the test would be as follows: first to enquire whether the party or group asserting the religious freedom qualifies as religious in order to assert the freedom. This is a threshold enquiry - not an enquiry into "core practices",but simply into whether religion exists, judged by sincerity of beliefs, surrounding symbols and practices. If no religion at all exists, there can be no protection under Article 25. If on the other hand, a religion does exist, the courts will then examine the law to see if the State has a compelling interest in enacting it. To answer this question, it will see whether the law is passed to give effect to the provisions of Part III, or made in the interest of public order, morality, health, regulating or restricting any economic, financial, political or other secular activity associated with religion, or is a measure of social reform. If the State's interest is compelling, the regulation stands; if it is not, the regulation fails.

National anthem case

To date, there appears to be only one case which has adopted this approach, namely *Bijoe Emmanuel vs. State of Kerala* (AIR 1987 SC 748). Children belonging to Jehovah's Witnesses were being compelled to sing the national antem on pain of expulsion from their school. They challenged this regulation as being violative of Article 25. Justice Chinnappa Reddy, after scanning the available literature, held that Jehovah's Witnesses truly and conscientiously believe what they say, do not hold their beliefs idly and their conduct was not the outcome of perversity. It was their belief that their religion does not permit them to join in any rituals except their prayer to Jehovah, their God. Hence religion existed and was entitled to protec-

tion. The Judge then proceeded to examine whether the ban imposed by the Kerala educational authorities was consistent with Article 25, i.e., whether it was required in the interest of maintaining public order, morality, health or the other provisions of Part III. This is how the test was formulated:

> We see that the right to freedom of conscience and freely to profess, practise and propagate religion guaranteed by Article 25 is subject to *(i)* public order, morality and health; *(ii)* other provisions of Part III of the Constitution; *(iii)* any law regulating or restricting any economic, financial, political or other secular activity which may be associated with religious practice; or *(iv)* providing for social welfare and reform or the throwing open of Hindu religious institutions of a public character to all classes and sections of Hindus. While on the one hand

Article 25 (1) itself expressly subjects the right guaranteed by it to public order, morality and health and to the other provisions of Part III, on the other, the State is also given the liberty to make a law to regulate or restrict any economic, financial, political or other secular activity which may be associated with religious practice and to provide for social welfare and reform, even if such regulation, resriction or provision affects the right guaranteed by Article 25 (1). Therefore, whenever the fundamental right to freedom of conscience and to profess, practice and propagate religion is invoked, the act complained of as offending the fundamental right must be examined to discover whether such act is to protect public order, morality and health, whether it is to give effect to the other provisions of Part III of the Constitution or whether it is authorised by a law made to regulate or restrict any economic, financial, political or secular activity which may be associated with religious practice or to provide for social welfare and reform. It is the duty and function of the Court so to do.

Having so formulated the test, the Court held that the expulsion of the children from the school because they conscientiously adhered to their religious faith and did not join in the singing of the national anthem is a violation of their fundamental right to freedom of conscience and the right to freely profess, practice and propagate religion.

Plight of tribal women

The non-interventionist attitude to family law on the ground that it is "private" not "public" has also led to indifference towards the plight of tribal women. Although ostensibly governed by customary law, in most cases they end up being governed by unreformed Hindu law; there is a general presumption that anyone who is not Christian or Muslim is Hindu. Thanks to the specific exclusion of tribals from the Hindu Succession Act (1955) and the Hindu Marriages Act, tribal women are governed by custom in matters relating to divorce, maintenance and inheritance. Thus, polygamy continues and tribal women do not inherit property which passes exclusively through the male line. The reasons for this non-interventionist attitude are not clear. While in pre-Independence India this would have been part of general British policy, in the post-Constitution period it was supposedly part of the policy to preserve the identity of tribal communities and ensure that their culture is not destroyed by non-tribals. Whereas this is entirely understandable regarding the alienation of tribal land to non-tribals, the application of unreformed Hindu law clearly dis-

criminates against tribal women and serves no purpose, social or otherwise.

Common element in all religions

In all religions, the father is the sole natural guardian of the child. Hindu law still gives to sons a birthright in ancestral property, to the exclusion of daughters. Muslim men may marry four wives, but their women may not marry more than one husband, whereas marriages of Hindus and Christians are expected to be monogamous. A Muslim woman cannot unilaterally divorce her husband whereas she can be so divorced by him. All divorced women are entitled to maintenance under Section 125 of the Criminal Procedure Code, but Muslim women, thanks to the Muslim Women's (Protection of Rights on Divorce) Act, 1986 are not. The right of a divorce for Christian women, compared to men, is so severely restricted that they virtually live in bondage.

In conclusion, one can state that the continued existence of anti-women, so-called "personal" laws, based on religion yet enforced by the State, is patently unconstitutional. Enforcing such laws in fact amounts to endorsing religious codes and sanctions and directly places the State and its judiciary in the position of final arbiter and defender of the faith.

Significant aspects of personal laws

Major efforts at codifying family laws were undertaken after Independence only for Hindus, between 1950-1956, when the Hindu Family Law was enacted. The Hindu Marriage Act was passed in 1955, and introduced the concept of monogamy and divorce for all Hindus. The term "Hindu" was defined widely to include all denominations of Hindus, Buddhists, Jains and Sikhs. Thus, the scope of the law was extensive and it covered the majority of India's population. All later statutes used the same definition of "Hindu". In 1956 the Hindu Succession Act was passed. It gave Hindu women — i.e. daughters, widows and wives of predeceased sons and the mother — equal rights to the self-acquired property of a Hindu male, dying intestate. It did not give a Hindu woman the right to become a co-parcener with her brother in her father's ancestral property. Although the Act was hailed as a milestone in conferring equal property rights on Hindu women, it excluded them from acquiring a share in ancestral property. Moreover, a Hindu male was free to make a will disinheriting his daughters, widow or mother.

The terms of the Act did not apply to agricultural property nor did they affect the operation of the law relating to fragmentation of agricultural holdings. Moreover, Section 23 of the Act prevents a Hindu family from demanding the partition of a dwelling place, and a Hindu woman has the right to reside in her ancestral home only if she remains unmarried.

The Hindu Adoption and Maintenance Act was passed in 1956, codifying the right of Hindus to adopt but only if the child is a Hindu; unmarried women, divorced women and widows have the right to adopt but married women do not; a Hindu male may adopt with the consent of his wife but a Hindu wife cannot. The Act also conferred on a Hindu woman the right to maintenance under certain circumstances. If her husband has deserted her, or treated her with cruelty, or if she has any other cause justifying her living separately, she can claim separate residence and maintenance. But this seemingly ben ficial right is subject to two very major exceptions; if she ceases to be a Hindu or if she is "unchaste," she has no right to maintenance. Her right is thus mediated both through her religion and through her sexuality. This law also gives a widowed daughter-in-law the right to maintenance by her father-in-law, provided she has no income or property, and is unable to obtain maintenance from the estate of her husband, her father or mother, her son or daughter or from their estates. The obligation of the father-in-law is limited to providing her maintenance out of co-parcenary property of which she has received her share.

In order to ask for maintainance the woman must to file a suit under this Act for which she has to pay a percentage of the amount claimed as maintenance, as court fees.

The Hindu Minority and Guardianship Act was passed in 1956. It states explicitly that the natural guardian of the minor children is the father and only then, the mother. The Act says that ordinarily the custody of a minor should be with the mother till the age of five. In the case of illegitimate children however, the natural guardian is the mother.

This is perhaps the single most discriminatory piece of legislation as it discriminates against the mother on grounds of sex alone. She cannot be the natural guardian of a child because *she is a woman*. Recently, the Law Commission recommended that the Act be amended to provide for general guardianship by both parents. This recommendation has not yet been acted upon. There have been several petitions in the Supreme Court challenging the constitutional validity of this provision but they have been put into cold storage and have remained undecided.

In 1976, the Hindu Marriage Act was amended to introduce divorce by mutual consent; simultaneously, the Special Marriages Act of 1954 was also similarly amended. At first, it appeared to be a progressive step, however, no attempt was made to ensure that the economic rights of a woman are safeguarded on breakdown of marriage. The year 1976 was a watershed in the history of Indian legislation; it was also the year in which the Special Marriages Act was amended so that Hindus married under it could continue to be governed by their personal law. This was a blatant attempt to transform a secular law into one which, for all practical purposes, was reverting back to religion. Whereas prior to this amendment Hindus married under the Special Marriages Act were governed by the Indian Succession Act, after it they were governed by the Hindu Succession Act.

Laws of marriage, divorce and succession relating to Christians were passed in the late nineteenth century by the British. The Indian Christian

Marriage Act was passed in 1862 and the Indian Divorce Act in 1869; both apply only to Indian Christians. The latter severely limits the right to divorce for a Christian woman — she must prove adultery, coupled with cruelty, desertion or bestiality to be entitled to a divorce. A Christian married man, on the other hand, has only to prove adultery.

Both laws were based on the then prevailing notions of marriage and divorce in English law and have remained static for over a century, although family laws in England have undergone progressive change. As mentioned earlier, although various courts have held that certain provisions of the Indian Divorce Act are at risk of being declared unconstitutional, and have directed the government to carry out necessary reforms, no attempts have been made to alter these Acts.

The Indian Succession Act was passed in 1865 and re-enacted in 1925. It is generally believed to be a secular law, but in fact, is applicable only to a person who is not a Hindu, Muslim, Sikh or Jain. In effect, therefore, it applies primarily to Christians and Jews (Parsis have their own law of succession) and its provisions are borrowed from the then prevailing laws of succession in England, as mentioned earlier. Until 1976, this Act also applied to those marrying under the Special Marriages Act (1954) when it was amended to ensure that Hindus who marry under this Act will continue to be governed by the Hindu Succession Act.

In effect the Indian Succession Act mainly governs Christians. Although sons and daughters have an equal share in the property belonging to their father, there is nothing in the Act which prevents a man from disinheriting his daughter. The experience of most women governed by this law has been that after the father's death, this is just what is likely to happen. In 1983, Mary Roy challenged the controversial Christian Succession Act which is applied to very wealthy Syrian Christians. It explicitly states that for a daughter the maximum amount of inheritence is Rs.5000. Mary Roy challenged it on grounds of discrimination; the Supreme Court upheld her submission and had the Act repealed in 1986.

The Guardians & Wards Act of 1890 relates to the appointment of a guardian for the person and property of a minor. It states that in appointing a guardian, the court shall be guided by the personal law to which the minor is subject, keeping in mind the welfare of the minor. In almost all personal laws, the father is the natural guardian of the child.

As far as Muslims are concerned, in matters of family inheritence, courts apply the law of the Koran. Civil regulations also empower courts to apply local customs regardless of race or religion. Such customs have led, in several instances, to demands from members of the Muslim community for restoration of Islamic law, and it was such a demand which led to the passing of the Shariat Act in 1937. This basically ensures that Muslim personal law is applied to matters relating to marriage, divorce, guardianship, dowry, maintenance, gifts, trusts, wakfs and inheritance (except in the case of agricultural land). Customary laws which applied to all communities, regardless of religion, were thus abrogated and replaced by Islamic law. The Dissolution of Muslim Marriages Act was passed in 1939 and gives Muslim women the right to demand divorce, as provided for in Hanafi law. Muslim women who did not have the right to divorce often converted to other religions, which automatically terminated their marriages. Alarmed by this tendency Muslim fundamentalists demanded the passing of a law to prevent conversion. The Act makes it clear that apostasy by women will not dissolve a marriage, whereas apostasy by a Muslim man does. After Independence no reform legislation relating to Muslims was undertaken, until the passing of the Muslim Women's (Protection of Rights on Divorce) Act, 1986.

—*Kirti Singh*

Women, Islamisation and justice

Shahla Zia

The Shariat Bill

As the final days approached before the debate on the Shariat Bill in the Pakistan National Assembly in May 1991, the women who had struggled against it for many years drew upon their last reserves of strength to try to prevent its passage. However, it was a losing battle and everyone knew it. And yet there was a refusal to accept its inevitability, an absurd hope that something would happen somewhere, somehow, to at least delay its passage. It is this kind of crazy hope that keeps the women's movement in Pakistan alive, for if this hope were abandoned what else would be left?

The Shariat Bill could be considered the final nail in the coffin. Even in its watered-down form it spells disaster for women — as does every law that has been passed in recent years in the name of Islam — and reverberations from the Bill, the final victory of the orthodox lobby, will be felt for years to come. Innocuous enough to allow many so-called liberals and progressives to salve their public consciences, it is a law that has come to stay.

But where did it all begin? Some date it to as recently as 1979 when General Zia-ul Haq passed his infamous Hadood Ordinances as part of his Islamisation campaign to justify his stay in power. Others suggest it originated in Bhutto's final days in power when he made a desperate attempt to appease the fundamenalists by banning liquor and declaring Friday the weekly holiday, thereby giving the nation a false notion of the power of the mullahs. Yet others believe it was in the early days of Constitution-making in Pakistan, when the Muslim League made concessions to the orthodoxy by compromising on constitutional provisions. Yet again, perhaps the issue was raised by the Muslim League in pre-Partition days in the interests of political expediency.

Whatever the debate on the socio-cultural, historical or political roots of oppression and the grossly unequal status of women in Pakistan, what is abundantly clear is that they have been treated badly by all sides. Socially disadvantaged and economically powerless, they have found that all types of laws and customs have militated against them. Traditional and customary law and practice have always relegated them to a subservient position. Personal law, religious in nature, has treated them as persons not quite equal, but deserving of kindness; labour law has considered them as persons requiring protection; and even secular law, reflecting as it did the biases and interests of a patriarchal system, did not help to elevate women's legal status. It did, however, allow them to at least sustain their position and hope for a better future, which was in itself a major achievement. But the move towards so-called Islamic law, across all civil and criminal codes, is what is proving to be the most damaging to women, further reinforcing their subordinate position whilst simultaneously creating a situation of extreme insecurity. Since this is happening through major changes in the judicial system and concepts of justice, the effects are likely to be far-reaching and incalculable.

The legal position

The legal position of women in Pakistan can neither be easily defined, nor assessed. Ordinarily this should be a fairly straightforward exercise: an examination of the Constitutional provisions and statutes that govern their constitutional, personal, labour, civic and political rights. But in Pakistan such an exercise would not only be inadequate, but misleading. Despite

Constitutional guarantees of equality, the Constitution itself carries provisions that serve to negate the fundamental right of equality and equal protection under the law. As well, laws exist and others are being enacted that are directly in conflict with the Constitution. And laws in the name of religion are subject to different interpretations, thereby causing even more confusion.

Moreover, when we try to assess women's legal status, which implies a more critical and qualitative analysis of their legal position, other factors come into play: do the laws safeguard the rights of women? Do they damage their status? Is there any conflict between the law and its practice? Is the law accompanied by the will to implement? And, finally, do the laws reflect women's interests and concerns?

Constitutional law

While the Fundamental Rights clearly lay down the equality of citizens and forbid discrimination on the basis of sex alone, certain other provisions of the Constitution have created situations that allow discrimination to continue. The provision that no law may be against the injunctions of the Koran and Sunnah has allowed a range of legislation that negates fundamental rights. The Council of Islamic Ideology and the Federal Shariat Court, both constitutionally created, have been and continue to be directly re-

تابیہ یہ دن کے جرم میں سزا کاٹ رہی ہے غریب والدین ضمانت کرانے کے قابل بھی نہیں ہیں

Girl to be tried under Zina Ordinance

By Our Staff Reporter

KARACHI Dec 21: A 16-year-old girl, who was abducted by five men and raped in confinement for over four months, has been charged under the Zina Ordinance (Enforcement of Hudood).

Manzooran alias Shameem, a servant girl working in Defence Housing Society interviewed in court, where she was brought for remand said she had gone out to throw trash when a group of men caught her and made her unconscious "by stuffing a handkerchief across my nose". She remembers being taken into a bus all the way to Kashmir. There she was reportedly beaten and raped by the abductors.

The young girl said she tricked one of her abductors, Gul Zaman, into bringing her back to Karachi by telling him she would ask her parents about his proposal for marriage. On landing at Sabzi Mandi bus stop, she told him she would raise hell if he touched her. Here, she boarded a rickshaw and landed home.

According to her, the abductors, acting in compliance with police, had her arrested. She was kept for 10 days in Saddar Police Station and charges have been made out against her under the Zina Ordinance (Section 10 and 11). Her brother, Iqbal Hussain who has filed the application on her behalf, alleged that the police had taken bribe. He said they had threatened the family not to mention the names of Haji Aziz and other kidnappers or else they would "be arrested in false criminal cases".

The DIG, police, has issued orders that the "case be investigated by a special investigation team". The Lawyers for Human Rights and Legal Aid has filed for bail for the release of the girl.

لاہور (جنگ نیوز) پشاور کی ایک جیل میں ایک 8 سالہ معصوم بچی ہیروئن کے جرم میں قید میں سزا کاٹ رہی ہے۔ معلوم ہوا ہے کہ اس بچی ناہید کے والدین اس قدر غریب ہیں کہ وہ اپنی لخت جگر کی ضمانت بھی نہیں کرا سکتے۔ یہ بچی نوشہ کے ایک محض نذیر کی بچی ہے اس بچی کے انصار بی بی نے جیل میں ملاقات کی اور بچی نے انہیں اپنی آپ بچی بتائی۔ پولیس کے مطابق اس لڑکی سے 500 گرام ہیروئن برآمد ہوئی تھی اور ہیروئن رکھنے کا الزام واحد اسی ایک بچی پر عائد کیا گیا ہے اور پولیس کی حراست میں تفتیش کی غرض سے ایک جسٹ لپٹ نے اس معصوم کا دو مرتبہ ریمانڈ لیا۔ اس سال 9 جنوری کو پولیس اس معصوم کو اس طرح ہتھکڑیاں پہنا کر جیل لائی جس طرح ہو بڑے بڑے خطرناک مجرموں کو لایا جاتا ہے۔

Gangrape: SI suspended

By Our Staff Reporter

LAHORE—Inspector-General of the Punjab Police, Ch Manzoor Ahmad, has suspended a Sub-Inspector, Mukhtar Shah of the Baghbanpura police for failing to register a case on the complaint of some locals.

According to a police handout, the victim of an alleged Baghbanpura gangrape did not mention of rape, they only reported about maltreatment. However, the SI did not register a case on the complaint.

The police, after three weeks of the incident, have registered 'a case under relevant laws'. Investigations are underway.

sponsible for some of the most retrogressive thoughts on women's rights, the former through its advice to the legislature and the latter through its judgements. Moreover, a number of laws exist that are in direct conflict with the Constitution. These include discriminatory laws like the Pakistan Citizenship Act (whereby the foreign wife of a Pakistani man is entitled to citizenship, but the foreign husband of a Pakistani woman is not), areas of personal law, portions of the labour laws, the Qanoon-e-Shahadat (that reduces the value of women's testimony to half that of a man's), the Hadood laws which oust the testimony of women altogether for the purposes of *hadd* punishment, and all the Islamic laws (which for purposes of inflicting punishment consider a girl child who has reached puberty to be an adult, while a boy is considered an adult at 18). Islamic laws morever, cannot be challenged as violating Fundamental Rights because of the Eighth Amendment to the Constitution that validates all ordinances, laws and acts made during the period of martial law and forbids their being questioned in any court of law, anywhere.

Personal laws

In matters of their personal rights, the law lays down that Muslims will be guided by their personal law, Shariat. While these have been important in codifying some rights for women they also highlight some inequalities and inequities. The law creates insecurity in marriage and divorce, since men have an absolute right of divorce and need not assign any reason for divorcing their wives. As well, women have no right to maintenance after divorce, no right to a share in marital property nor the right to live in the marital home. Not only do women not have an absolute right to divorce, they can only gain that right *if* the husband agrees to delegate it. Inequality of access to legal remedies is another disability since women have to prove their divorce cases in court, while men merely have to send a notice. Personal law also offers women inadequate legal protection, as laws prohibiting child marriage and placing restraints on second marriages are ineffective; women continue to regard such marriages as valid despite violations of the law. Financial insecurity is similarly built in, since women's property inheritance is rarely granted them, particularly in agricultural societies where customary law prevails.

In practice, many of the laws favourable to women have been ignored and their implementation been ineffective. Judicial interpretations, that in earlier periods played an important role in securing rights for women, have become increasingly orthodox in response to the political climate.

Labour laws

While labour laws have some protective or beneficial provisions for women (prohibition against night work, certain types of work, maternity benefits, etc.), they also provide examples of discrimination against them. Protective legislation leads to job discrimination, since it denies women employment in certain specified areas. It also leads to lower scales of pay since the work they are assigned is often classified as low-skill; and protective/beneficial provisions are regarded as concessions, not condition-related rights. In practice, many female workers do not receive the benefits due to them. The provision of benefits can also lead to job insecurity because employers often keep women on as temporary workers to avoid paying maternity benefits. Moreover, since a substantial proportion of women workers belongs to the informal sector, they are not covered by any of the labour laws and are subject to exploitation.

Islamic laws

Laws passed in the name of religion have proved to be amongst the most damaging for women. These include the Hadood Ordinances, the Qanoon-e-Shahadat, the Qisas and Diyat Ordinance and the Shariat Bill. Blatantly discriminatory, they have drastically diminished women's constitutional rights as equal citizens by reducing the value of their testimony in certain civil matters and discounting it altogether when awarding certain criminal penalties. Unforgiveably, they have equated the offence of rape (a crime of violence) with adultery (a victimless offence) for the purpose of quantum of evidence, thus making a charge of rape almost impossible to prove. Judgements of the Federal Shariat Court have further threatened women by making it possible for them to be convicted of adultery if they are unable to prove their charges of rape. In awarding penalties, the laws have changed the definition of adult for females to cover all girls who have reached puberty, placing young girls in grave danger. The Qisas and Diyat Ordinance has changed the whole concept of criminal accountability in the justice system, and the Shariat Bill has created ambiguities that allow social biases and retrogressive thought to resurface. For women, this implies a denial of their constitutional right to equality and equal legal protection, a restriction on their right to prosecute, the very real danger of increased violence against them since cases of rape are impossible to prove, and increased insecurity because their rights and personal safety are threatened both by new interpretations of the laws and the dangers created by ambiguity.

Effects on women

Policies of the State in Pakistan have

Innocent woman, her children get bail after 7 years

Sakina who spent 7½ years in Karachi Central Prison along with her two children on the charge of Zina (Hadood Ordinance) has been quitted from the case by the Additional District and Sessions Judge Central Shamsuddin Hisbani. Her case was argued and fought by Zia Ahmad Awan Advocate, President Lawyers for Human Rights and Legal Aid on behalf of Sakina on purely humanitarian grounds.

Sakina was sent to jail by North Nazimabad police along with her two children, Nasreen 10 and Danish 8½ on the complaint of her father who lodged a report in July 1980 with North Nazimabad police station accusing his son-in-law Hazoor Bux for abducting his married daughter Sakina with the intention of Zina.

The police arrested both Hazoor Bux and Sakina and produced them before the magistrate. Thereafter in the light of statement made by Sakina, the police implicated her with Hazoor Bux under Zina Hadood Ordinance. After 7½ years in jail she made an application to President LHRLA in which she mentioned that she had been forced to marry twice on the consideration of money by her father and brother. When she refused to marry 3rd time and took shelter with her brother-in-law Hazoor Bakhsh, her father became annoyed with both of them and lodged a false compalain.

According to Sakina, she considers Hazoor Bux as her father. The LHRLA took up her case about five months back and got her released from jail with the help of Abdus Sattar Edhi who furnished bail amount of Rs 10,000/- for Sakina. The LHRLA also offered Hazoor Bux for bail but he has refused to come out on bail, as he is under fear of death from the complainant. Sakina after release on bail preferred to live in Edhi Centre Clifon with her two children.

Umrani, Secretary Sindh Land Commission is transferred and posted with immediate effect as A.D.M. Kotri, vice Mr. Manzoor Ali Awan transferred; Mr. Anzar Hussain Zaidi is posted with immediate effect as Deputy Secretary Education; and Mr Ghulam Rasool Kalwar, Deputy Secretary Education is transferred and posted in his own pay and scale with immediate effect as Additional Commissioner-I, Sukkur against existing vacancy.

usually failed to make a connection between social justice and the law. While the delivery of social justice obviously extends beyond the domain of law, it must be recognised that the legal rights of people are central to achieving any measure of justice at all. When law itself creates social injustices, the issue takes a very serious turn.

Legislation that denies equality to women limits their choices and reinforces their subordination. A major example is the Qanoon-e-Shahadat that states that, in the event of future and financial transactions being reduced to writing, the acceptable testimony would be that of two men or one man and two women. Because of the absurdity of the situation it created, the law was largely ignored, but it was hazardous to women, particularly working women. Its effects are being felt today in, for example, the banking profession where the promotion of women officers is involved. Since the Shariat Bill was passed these effects have been more acute. In a number of cases in Islamabad registration authorities have refused to accept the signatures of women attesting documents, demanding that male witnesses be produced. The laws of Hadood have diminished the personal status of women where, although otherwise recognised as a *sui juris* agent, a woman loses that legal capacity as a witness in Hadood cases.

Projection of women's subordinate image

These laws which are welfare-oriented, rather than rights-oriented have a definite impact on other aspects of women's lives. In their work, they are always regarded as less capable; in their daily lives, the few rights they have are rarely taken seriously or implemented by concerned agencies; in the political arena, their concerns are seldom addressed or reflected. A major example of this subordinate status is personal laws, which declare the father to be the natural guardian of children; it further always takes the position of a man *giving* a divorce, a woman *taking* one, by itself a subordinating mechanism. The provision of maintenance based on women's dependent status rather than in recognition of their contribution to the marriage, only reinforces this. Protective legislation in labour laws which, recognising the reproductive role of women, protect them from working at night and from performing certain jobs, is undertood negatively. Finally labour legislation requires that compensation to a deceased workman's heirs if they are minors, insane or women, will not be handed over in a lump-sum.

Insecurity for women

Recent laws passed in the name of religion have not only created a high degree of insecurity for women, they have made for considerabe ambiguity about their legal status. For example, the Hadood laws pertaining to rape have resulted in greater violence against women. They have increased women's involvement in the criminal injustice system without providing any protective mechanisms against violence. Decisions of the higher courts that have denied girls their right to choice in marriage against the wishes of their family, have affected their *sui juris* status. The decisions of the Federal Shariat Court in rape cases where women victims have instead been tried and convicted for adultery, have in fact, perpetuated injustice. Not only are they unable to secure justice for the crimes committed against them, they are further threatened for daring or presuming to make an issue of it. All the penal Islamic laws have created immense danger for women by redefining their adulthood in terms of being guilty and receiving punishment. Under the Majority Act, both boys and girls are considered adults upon reaching the age of 18, but under Islamic laws a girl is presumed to be an adult when she acquires puberty. This means that while the value of her evidence in civil matters is only half that of man's and is totally discounted for the purpose of hard punishments, she is adult enough at puberty to receive *the maximum punishment under law*. The Qisas and Diyat Ordinance which subscribes to the concept of crime being an offence against individuals, not society, poses other serious threats to women's security. There has already been a case where a husband murdered his wife and children (the heirs) but the law forgave him for the crime, allowing him to go unpunished. In a country where there is a history of subjugation of women and where marital abuse of wives is accepted, this places women in extreme jeopardy.

The full impact of the Shariat Bill is yet to be properly assessed, but its effects are already perceptible. The issue of whether a woman can be head of state was once again raised by members of the highest legislative forums, where threats to non-*mehram* women were also voiced. At the judicial level, in a case where a man had murdered his wife claiming he had caught her in the act of adultery, he was granted bail on the grounds that now that Shariat was in force, Mufti Naeemi's ruling that a man has a right to kill his wife if caught committing adultery, had to be upheld.

Beneficial laws inadequately implemented

Those laws which extend some benefits to women are seldom implemented effectively, primarily because of existing socio-cultural biases reflected in the administrative, judicial and enforcement branches, but also because of legal and procedural inadequacies. Despite the Child Marriages

کوئٹہ ارب علی خان (نامہ نگار) پولیس کی مہینہ زیادتی کے خلاف احتجاج کرنیوالے دیہاتیوں جلوس پر پولیس نے فائرنگ کردی جس سے ایک شخص موقع پر ہلاک اور تین افراد شدید زخمی ہوگئے جن میں ایک لڑکی بھی شامل ہے تفصیلات کے مطابق الیس اچاؤ تھانہ برنالہ جاوید گیلانی اور کانسٹیبل عبدالغفور کو گزشتہ دنوں موضع دہوزاں والا کے ایک شخص نامر عرف ناصرہ نے اپنے گھر میں قتل کردیا تھا اس روز سے پولیس نے موضع دہوزاں والا' مندرپور اور تاؤ میں اپنے کیمپ لگا رکھے ہیں اور مہینہ طور پر مختلف لوگوں سے زیادتیاں کررہے ہیں کذشتہ شب جب گاؤں کی ایک لڑکی سے ایک پولیس ملازم نے مہینہ بندر رینہ کالا کرنے کی کوشش کی تواس کے شور پر گاؤں میں بہت کھچ لوگ اکٹھے ہوگئے اور احتجاجی جلوس کی شکل میں سماجی رہنما کرنل عبدالغنی کے پاس بر ہلا جانے لگے تو پولیس نے موضع کوٹ جیل کے قریب جلوس پر اندھا دھند فائرنگ

Sentence set aside

SAHIWAL, April 11: The Federal Shariat Court has set aside the 14 year R.I., 20 lashes and Rs 5,000 fine-sentence awarded to a zamindar of Noor Shah, Taj Mohammed, and ordered his release.

The Additional Sessions Judge, Sahiwal, Syed Ijaz Hussain Rizvi, it may be added, had awarded this punishment to the zamindar on Nov. 17, 1984 for kidnapping and criminally assaulting a girl. The zamindar later filed a petition against the verdict of the Sessions Court in Federal Shariat Court which accepted the petition.—PPI

Girl, paramour awarded jail term, fine and lashes

From Our Correspondent

MUZAFFARGARH, Feb 18: The Additional District and Sessions Judge, Muzaffargarh, Alhaj Ferozuddin, has awarded 29 years rigorous imprisonment and ten lashes to a young girl, Rasheeda of Shah Jamal, while her paramour, Muhammad Hussain, was sentenced to 6 years rigorous imprisonment, 20 lashes and fine Rs 1000. The girl would have to undergo further nine months imprisonment in default of payment of fine of Rs 2,500. She was tried on the charge of murder, developing indecent ties, while her paramour was tried under Zina Ordinance.

According to the prosecution, one Rasheeda of village Sharif Chhajra (Shah Jamal) murdered a six-year-old boy, Muhammad Asghar, son of Muhammad Hussain, to avenge her insult from her paramour, who subjected her to criminal assaults several times with the promise to marry her.

When she insisted on fulfilling the promise, he flatly refused to do so.

Then she planned to take revenge of insult and slaughtered his son, Asghar. The court awarded her life term and fined Rs 2,000 for killing a minor boy, four years R.I. ten lashes and a fine of Rs. 500 under the Zina Ordinance.

Restraint Act, such marriages continue to take place without deter or penalty. Though the Family Laws Ordinance has laid down a procedure by which second marriages can be contracted, it is widely disregarded and no action taken for violation. Delay in the dispensation of justice prevents women from asserting their rights. The fact that many critical areas of family dispute (for instance, dowry, marital gifts, property, etc.) are not within the jurisdiction of the family courts, also creates problems since cases then become too expensive for women to institute. The laws themselves are also weak in their implementation and penalty clauses, thus rendering them ineffective. No administrative measures have been taken to alleviate women's problems, nor are there sufficient support services — shelters, day-care centres, legal aid and counselling — to help them through critical periods of distress.

Attempted changes and concepts of justice

The introduction of religious laws has re-opened the debate on women's rights which had been contained under secular law. Since the most vocal group on the subject of women is the orthodox lobby, there is bound to be sustained damage to the status of women. The Shariat Bill, by being made the supreme law in contradiction to the Constitution, is a major instrument in this. Ambiguous laws invariably serve the interests of the orthodoxy. For instance, the passing of the Qisas and Diyat Ordinance seeking to change the entire concept of crime and accountability; the setting up of the Federal Shariat Court as a parallel judiciary responsible to the executive; and the working of forums like the Council of Islamic Ideology and the Federal Shariat Court which are the domain of fundamentalists.

Most of the laws discussed have been recommended by the all-male Council of Islamic Ideology, passed by a heavily male-dominated assembly and interpreted by an all-male Federal Shariat Court. As such, they reflect only the interests of the orthodoxy and their insensitivity to gender concerns. The only law passed since the creation of Pakistan on the recommendation of women is the Family Laws Ordinance, although even here their recommendations were not fully incorporated.

Future directions

The major concern for women in Pakistan today is not merely overcoming the existing socio-legal problems and hindrances, but anticipating and fighting against all the possible ramifications of Islamic laws. The question arises: what can women do about it? While previous strategies adopted by the women's movement may have been effective in bringing the women's question to the fore, in mobilising support and in contributing to the watering-down of proposed laws, they have not been able to prevent the State from making major changes. Compounding the problem is the changed political environment: there is no longer an obvious enemy like an authoritarian or martial law-cum-fundamentalist government, to fight against. Nevertheless, valuable lessons have been learnt both through successes and failures and the fight is still on at many levels and on many fronts. As important as a change of attitude is for the women's movement to stop feeling defensive about its existence. This has in the past, often led to a constant anxiety about image (do we come across as urban, elitist, militant, un-Islamic etc.?), resulting in an attempt to conform to an image prescribed for them by society. What is important is for people to see that the interests being represented are those of all women, not of any one class or section. This can only be done by forging strong links with all women's groups fighting against oppression, and by emphasising their commonalities.

Another important step for the women's movement is to change its position of powerlessness. Had it been powerful enough to cripple the government for even one day, as the truck-drivers did when the Qisas and Diyat Ordinance was passed, many a so-called sacred law would have been overturned. As a strategy the women's movement will have to establish closer ties with other oppressed or neglected groups as well as with rights-oriented organisations like trade unions, minorities, peasants, the Left, human rights groups, etc, to strengthen their mutual positions.

The movement must also maintain a strong public profile in its continued fight for recognition. Active lobbying and pressure groups are essential to ensure that their concerns are noticed. In the case of the Shariat Bill, while the personal lobbying with legislators began only a few days prior to the debate in the National Assembly, it resulted in some important inclusions concerning women in the Bill. More importantly those few days of hectic lobbying ensured that every person who spoke on the Bill had perforce to address the women's issue; this included the Treasury Benches. Simultaneous with the passing of the Bill, the Prime Minister appointed a woman as Advisor, an obvious effort to appease women and send out a message that the Bill would not affect them adversely.

Pressure on policy makers must also be sustained. The movement cannot afford to sit back and relax in the hope that sympathetic persons or governments will take appropriate action on their behalf. The women's issue is not a priority for any government; in fact, it is a subject that most of them would prefer to shelve because of its controversial nature. An obvious example is that of the People's Party government which, despite its manifesto, did nothing to repeal the several discriminatory laws during its stint in power.

At the same time pressure must be kept up on all political parties to take up the women's issue as one relevant to them. For any long-term effectiveness, however, ways must be found of ensuring that political parties have a sufficient number of women members generally, and especially at the executive or policy making level. Finally the movement must recognise that its chances of success for justice within the existing system are seriously limited. Ultimately its only hope of achieving its goal lies in a secular system of government; a total separation of State and religion.

Illustrations are from *Rape in Pakistan* (Simorgh Women's Resource and Publication Centre, Lahore).

The Shariat Bill and its impact on education and women

Rubina Saigol

God is for men and religion for women. *saiell*

Historical background

Beginning with the Pakistan National Alliance movement against Zulfiqar Ali Bhutto's government, there has been a continuous trend towards right-wing, religious, fundamentalist thought in the military-bureaucratic establishment in Pakistan. Capitalising on the popular unrest with Bhutto's government, Zia-ul Haq, the military dictator, appropriated a backward, Jamaat-e-Islami brand of fundamentalist Islam and put it to use to legitimise his illegal rule. Declaring himself to be divinely appointed to fulfil the task of Islamising the country, he began a massive campaign to cleanse society of un-Islamic practices and vices. Women, minorities and other relatively powerless groups became the prime target of his drive against anything he and the ulema defined as anti-Islam. The small number of progressive legal and other reforms, such as the Family Laws Ordinance of 1961, began to be challenged.

Over a period of five to seven years major changes in the legal structure of the country significantly lowered the status of women in society. The Hadood Ordinance, the Law of Evidence and several other pieces of legislation had an unmistakeably anti-female bias; given the strongly conservative and repressive political and legal environment created in the country, the atmosphere of fear, insecurity and oppression that resulted had a direct impact on women. Conservative thinking began to permeate all sections of society but was most visible in the mass media and education — the two areas in which women had high visibility and were competing successfully against men. Right-wing ideologues who had never gained power directly through elections here saw their chance to gain control over ideology, over *what* people think and *how* they think. During Zia's rule sweeping changes were made in academic curricula to bring them in line with Islamic values and thought, and students were systematically indoctrinated with religious prejudice in the guise of science and learning.

After Zia-ul Haq's death in 1988 there was a perceptible change in the political atmosphere of the country, but the retrogressive legislation curtailing women's rights remained intact. Zia's legacy continued to exist as the military-bureaucratic establishment had become strongly politicised and infused with right-wing ideas. Religious fundamentalism continued to exert an influence over all aspects of social and cultural life.

The Sami-Latif Bill, May 1990[1]

In May 1990 the Senate (upper house of parliament) which was heavily dominated by Zia's ideological successors, passed a private members' bill, moved by Maulana Sami-ul Haq and Qazi Abdul Latif, relating to the imposition of Shariat. Its passage in the Senate was part of the chain of laws and ordinances designed to make Pakistan a theocratic State. Although the bill dealt with the overall Islamisation of society and the imposition of Shariat in every area of activity, it specifically mentioned four that would be directly affected: the economy, mass media, the judicial system, and education. Certain aspects of the economy were removed from its immediate control to provide the government with an escape clause in financial matters,[2] but the other three clearly indicate the attempt by the religious right to gain virtual monopoly over the legal and ideological machinery of the State.

The judiciary

The bill contained various provisions that would cripple the judicial system and the Constitution by making the muftis and mullahs, directly appointed by the President, extremely powerful vis-a-vis the judges of the regular law courts. These semi-literate muftis, whose educational qualifications were well below those required for regular legal practice, could declare any law or governmental action repugnant to Islam and thus hamper the legislative and administrative functioning of the State. Additionally, these provisions gave the President undue power in a parliamentary form of government, and also enabled the judiciary to legislate rather than merely interpret the law. Moreover, it was unclear whose interpretation of Shariat would prevail since not only do different sects interpret it differently, the same sect may also sometimes disagree internally. Although the personal laws of the minorities were to be left untouched, they would be subject to Shariat in the political and economic spheres.[3]

Progressive sections of society soon realised that the Islamisation of education meant that anything in curricula which conflicted with the mullah's interpretation of Islam would be removed, thus inhibiting the pursuit of knowledge and the quest for a scientific and analytical understanding of nature and society. Media would also be put to use in the service of religious and obscurantist interests. An endless spate of moral sermons would be dished out, with a near total absence of any alternate, progressive or secular perspective.

In all this women, especially the less privileged, would be affected more directly because they are in competition with newly urbanised, conservative youth in the universities and have high visibility in the media. The thrust towards Islamisation (and Islamic punishments in particular) has been seen to affect the underprivileged classes, women and minorities, in particular.[4]

On account of these regressive provisions a concerted movement was launched against the Shariat Bill. The Women's Action Forum (WAF) called a meeting of progressive intellectuals, minority leaders, women's organisations and lawyers to form a joint front to oppose the passage of the bill in the National Assembly; the Joint Action Committee for People's Rights, comprising 40 organisations, was formed as a result. It represented human, women's and minorities'

rights, and anyone interested in a just and democratic order. The Joint Action Committee held seminars and protest meetings, published pamphlets and articles and sent letters to members of the National Assembly to convince them of the far-reaching implications of the bill, of how it would curb women's rights, violate the Constitution, erode the independence of the judiciary and curtail the law-making power of legislators.

In October 1990 Nawaz Sharif took over as the Islami Jamhoori Ittehad prime minister and came under pressure from right-wing elements in his alliance to enforce Shariat in the country. By this time however, there was nationwide agitation against the proposed bill and some maulanas within his own alliance disagreed with its provisions, on the ground that they were not Islamic enough. In an effort to appease the religious right without at the same time bringing about the destruction of political institutions, the IJI government passed a watered down version of the bill in May 1991.[5] The government-sponsored official Shariat Bill passed by the Assembly in 1991 retained some aspects of the original Sami-Latif bill in that it proposed the imposition of Shariat, but added that this would be interpreted by each sect according to its tenets. The bill attempted to reduce the influence of the religious right by greatly diluting the powers granted to legally untrained muftis; it repeated certain provisions already laid down in the Resolution of Objectives and left many areas vague and open to wide variations in interpretation. This very vagueness, however, was its most dangerous aspect as its many clauses could be interpreted by the establishment in any way it chose.

Control of education and the media

Education and mass media were once again specified in the bill as being in need of Islamisation. The religious right is fully cognizant of the fact that controlling ideology is a powerful means of controlling society, and education is the most efficient means of transmitting ideas. An earlier generation of students was less influenced by right-wing thought as Pakistan had newly emerged from colonial rule and was still heavily dominated by liberal English traditions of thought.

Early leaders too, like M.A. Jinnah, were basically secular and modern. During Ayub Khan's era progressive ideas still prevailed as most army officers were generally liberal in their ideology, and Ayub Khan had his own differences with the religious right. Students were more influenced by progressive and left ideas and participated in large numbers in Bhutto's apparently socialist movement against Ayub.

After the takeover of the government by General Zia-ul Haq, the fundamentalist Jamaat-e-Islami, which has never won support among the masses, infiltrated the institutions of state power in substantial numbers and gained a disproportionate influence in affairs of state. For the first time in the history of the country retrogressive ideas and laws against women were initiated by the govern-

ment in power. There arose demands for segregating women's education, pushing them back into their homes and confining them to the domestic and reproductive spheres.

During Zia's regime all modern, liberal, scientific ideas were removed from academic curricula in favour of the glorification of Islam and of the military; Zia used education to the hilt to promote his ideas and legitimise his rule. Due to the ban on all political activity during his regime, student politics became the only arena for political struggle; the religious right exploited this situation fully to entrench itself in the universities and gain control of the highly vulnerable students. Further, progressive parties were too preoccupied with sur-

viving under martial law to organise a progressive student movement, with the result that religious parties walked right in. With the liberal and left-wing political parties under constant persecution, the burden of opposing Zia's repressive order fell mainly on women, who assumed this responsibility under the umbrella of Women's Action Forum.

The Shariat Bill, education and women

Let us now look specifically at the official Bill passed by the IJI government in May 1991 and examine its implications for education in the following areas: *(i)* content and implementation of curricula; *(ii)* science and the spirit of critical inquiry; *(iii)* de-

Syllabi to conform to Islam

ISLAMABAD, April 6, (APP): Federal Government has taken a number of steps to bring the syllabi of the educational institutions in conformity with Islam and ideology of Pakistan.

These steps include: Introduction of Islamiat and Pakistan Studies as compulsory subjects from class 1 to BA/BSc level and corresponding to professional degrees and other programmes.

Contributions of early Muslim thinkers have been highlighted in sciences and associated subjects.

Relevant Islamic concepts have been incorporated in curriculum and textbooks of each subject. For example, economics course includes Islamic concept of economics.

More than 500 titles of textbooks for class 1 to XII were reviewed by highly skilled experts committees in early 80s and the material which was considered repugnant to Islam and ideology of Pakistan was replaced by appropriate modifications.

All the courses are continuously being reviewed and updated to incorporate appropriate material on the teachings and ideology of Islam as research and advanced studies bring about new knowledge and findings.[7]

mocracy and democratic institutions; *(iv)* social and political consciousness; and *(v)* education of women.

We will first take up the issue of changes in the curriculum. Point 6(a) of the bill states that "The State shall make effective arrangements for teaching of and training in the Shariat, Islamic jurisprudence and all other branches of Islamic law at appropriate levels of education and professional training; (b) include courses on the Shariat in the syllabi of the law colleges; and (c) teach the Arabic language." Point number 7, referring to the Islamisation of education, states:

"The State shall take necessary steps to ensure that the educational system of Pakistan is based on Islamic values of learning, teaching and character-building."[6]

It is not difficult to see that taken together these provisions will make curricula completely ideological. Although law and professional training have been specifically mentioned, all subjects will be taught from a purely one-dimensional Islamic viewpoint; no debate, argument, disagreement or alternative view will be allowed to prevail, not even other Islamic interpretations. One fears that history, for example, is and will be taught in a way in which communal hatred and prejudice will increase since all Muslim rulers and conquerors will be presented as heroes, regardless of their oppression, and all non-Muslims will be presented as villains, despite their greatness. Muslim conquests and monarchies will be glorified and eulogised thereby encouraging a feudal/monarchical consciousness; such a consciousness in turn is usually unwilling to accept or understand democratic and egalitarian ideas.

This proposed Islamisation adds to the enormous amount of Islamic content already present in the Punjab Textbook Board Curriculum, especially in the Urdu, Islamiat, Pakistan studies and history courses. A quick statistical analysis of the Urdu curriculum published in January 1990[8] reveals that 23 per cent of all topics from classes 1 to VIII deal directly with religion. These include Hamd, Naat, the character of the Prophet, and Islamic values and morality such as obedience, submissiveness and docility. Another 18 per cent deal with nationalistic, patriotic and militaristic ideas such as Our Flag, Our National Anthem, Our Army, Military Medals and Military Heroes, values of martyrdom and the glorification of the State. This content is strongly reinforced with underpinnings of religious ideology, while love for the State and glorification of the army are linked to the protection of Islam. The curriculum thus becomes one of Islamic, militaristic nationalism.

As one progresses to the higher classes, from class VI to class VIII, the religious content increases by one-third and the militaristic-nationalistic content doubles.

As students grow older they are fed with increasing doses of religious and militaristic ideology which effectively suppresses critical or reflective thinking by promoting a monolithic concept of truth. By contrast the total percentage of scientific topics in the entire Urdu curriculum is 3.3 per cent, an abysmally low figure when we consider that religious, national and "moral" content together constitute roughly 75 per cent of the curriculum. In history, there is only one chapter on the contribution of women to the Pakistan Movement and none on the concept of democracy. Topics on science do not increase at the higher levels; there is generally only one chapter in each book on a scientific topic such as radar, TV, telephones and the Apollo mission.

This brief survey covers only the Urdu curriculum. Pakistan studies, history, Islamiat and even the sciences have a generous sprinkling of Islamic content, and even secular subjects have a strong undertone of so-called Islamic values. With the compulsory addition of Arabic to the curriculum, the dream of our policy makers to identify with Saudi Arabia will be fulfilled. The holy warriors of

education have launched a crusade against all progressive thought and scientific knowledge by removing virtually all rational content from textbooks, replacing it with what seeks inspiration from "holy" sources in foreign lands. The irony lies in the fact that we hope to carve a national identity from non-national sources.

Science a casualty

The second major casualty of the Islamisation of education will be science, whose worldview is opposed to religious doctrines. A religious party in Islamabad is preparing a science curriculum according to which children will be taught that when two atoms of hydrogen and one atom of oxygen are chemically mixed the re-

sult will be water *if Allah's will is added to the mixture*. When physics and chemistry are thus made into a mockery we can imagine the kind of understanding of the physical universe that will be inculcated in the minds of the young.

Now, in order to create an industrial culture, science and technology are essential; yet technical knowledge without an understanding of the basic principles of inquiry and analysis becomes arid technicism which creates robots who follow the rules without questioning their origin or purpose.

Impact upon democracy

The third major area to be seriously

I KNEW IT! HE'S NOT IN HIS GRAVE!!

affected by this control over ideology by the State will be our already crippled democracy. Education has historically been put to use to serve the interests of the ruling elites. Prior to the advent of the British in India, indigenous forms of education were used to extol the virtues of the Mughals and to glorify monarchy. The British anglicised and secularised Indian education in the first half of the nineteenth century in order to produce a class of local administrators who would mimic the Englishman but be cheaper than the officers of the East India Company. This education also served the purpose of ideologically tying the interests of the wealthy and privileged Indian classes to British imperial interests. The East

India Company showed no interest in educating the Indian masses for fear of rebellion resulting from enhanced awareness. Initially the Muslims of India remained aloof from English education which they perceived as antithetical to Islam; however Sir Syed Ahmad Khan soon introduced the idea to upper class Muslims that without it they would, as a community, fall behind the Hindu upper classes in obtaining coveted civil service jobs. Sir Syed not only brought communal separation into Indian education, he also opposed the education of the masses and women.[9] His educational ideas were fundamentally undemocratic and were meant to serve only upper class Muslim youth.[10] His Aligarh movement helped in the production of an educated and westernised elite which prided itself on its differentiation from the masses; this elite eventually formed the Muslim League to protect and promote its economic and political interests against Hindu competitors. However, since the rallying slogan for Pakistan was the creation of a Muslim nation (as the masses could not be expected to fight to protect landlord interests), many people still believe that Pakistan was created solely for the protection of Islam. This myth has given rise to the recurring spectre of fundamentalism in post-Partition Pakistan.

The present Establishment - the military-bureaucratic oligarchy as it is often called - and our landowning and capitalist classes are once again using the same strategy against the people. It sends its own children to private schools so that they have the benefit of a more varied and democratic curriculum, will take a foreign qualifying exam, travel west for their higher education, and return to occupy positions of power and privilege in the bureaucracy, the army and private enterprise, thus completing the circle.

The State will ensure its stability and power by providing the children of the lower and lower middle classes a government education in which the curriculum will teach them the "Islamic" values of obedience, docility, submissiveness and subordination, ensuring that they keep their position of subordination in the social hierarchy. The values of loyalty to the State, patriotism, love for the military, so dominant in the official curriculum, will preclude any opposition to the State because such opposition will inevitably be construed as anti-national and un-Islamic. The theocratic State, based on the power of the elite, will thus protect itself from any possible agitation or rebellion. The educational provisions of the Shariat Bill are therefore an insidious way of reproducing the class cultural power of the dominant classes and the ideology of subordination for the underprivileged.

This is the reason why there has been a de-emphasis in recent education policies, on the teaching of history, economics, sociology and political science, which create an awareness of social inequality and oppression.[11] The emphasis on technical training without an accompanying stress on the social sciences will produce an uncritical technicist mentality, highly suitable for exploitative working conditions. This strategy will enable the ruling elite to produce a middle and lower level, technically competent, but politically docile working class for industry.

Impact upon women's education

The segregation of education along gender lines is another feature of current policies. Separate universities and colleges for women will be set up which will inculcate values of obedience and docility, and notions of Islamic morality will be used to justify their subordinate status. The cult of domesticity will be encouraged through the teaching of domestic sciences, and a downscaling of so-called "hard" sciences. This will seriously limit the options available to women in career terms; they will find themselves channelled into low-status, low-income jobs which become even more so as they become "feminised". It is also likely that women's educational institutions will be lower on the priority list for funding as their education is traditionally regarded as less important than men's.

Other provisions of the Bill will also adversely affect women's status. For example, it says that the State shall "take effective legal and administrative measures to eradicate obscenity, vulgarity and other moral vices", prostitution being one of them.[12] As in Zia's regime, women are still likely to be the main targets of the obscenity drive, and many will be punitively punished for prostitution without any questioning of the social conditions which promote and perpetuate it. What is particularly alarming is the proposed setting up of a task force of volunteers who will invade people's homes to "inspect" their morality! Such a voyeuristic police state is contrary to all universally accepted norms of democracy, justice, personal liberty and the right to privacy.

The social and political climate created during Zia's rule through the Hadood Ordinance, the Law of Evidence, and other discriminatory legislation was one of oppression and violence against women. That climate is being recreated with the passage of the official Shariat Bill; the drive to repeal the Family Laws Ordinance, to push urban women out of the formal sector, to propagate domesticity as a virtue, to establish the superiority of men, to force purdah upon women, to segregate and undermine their education, to represent them in traditional roles in the media, and other retrogressive measures are all signs of the institutionalisation of discriminatory practices.

In conclusion, let us take a quick look at the terminology of the present Bill. "And whereas Islam has been declared to be the State religion of Pakistan and thus it has become obligatory for all Muslims to follow the injunctions of the Holy Quran and Sunnah to regulate and order their lives in complete submission to the Divine law."[13] The significant phrase here is "has become obligatory for all Muslims", for the element of coercion is clearly present. Point number 5 states, "All Muslim citizens of Pakistan shall order their lives according to the Shariat," while the Constitution of 1973 stated that all Muslims would be enabled to order their lives according to their beliefs. There is a crucial difference between "shall order" or "has become obligatory" and "being enabled".The question is: Who will interpret what divine law is? In all likelihood it will be the mullahs who decide and who will define "the wishes and aspirations of the people of Pakistan" in accordance with a set of principles and dictates that militate against democratic, progressive practice.

Cartoons reproduced from the Simorgh Diary (Lahore, 1994.).

Notes

[1] See the text of the Sami-Latif private members' bill, 1990; *The Shariat Bill and Its Implications,* Human Rights Commission of Pakistan (Lahore: Lighthouse Press).

[2] Ibid, p. 10.

[3] Ibid, p.2.

[4] See A. Jahangir and Hina Jilani's *The Hadood Ordinances: A Divine Sanction?* (Lahore: Rohtas Books, 1990).

[5] See the text of the government sponsored official Shariat Bill, 1991, as it appeared in *The News*, April 12, 1991.

[6] Ibid. point 7.1.

[7] See *Frontier Post*, April 7, 1991.

[8] See the Urdu curriculum prepared by the Punjab Textbook Board,1990.

[9] See Khutbat-e-Sir Syed, vol.2. Majlis-e-Taraqqi-e-Adab, Lahore. The following is a translation by the author of Sir Syed's extract on women's education: "There is no doubt that I disapprove of the establishment of schools where girls congregate in veils and `chadars' irrespective of the family or social class they belong to.

"Who knows what kind of company they must keep at such places? Who knows what kind of girls collect in such establishments? Who knows what kind of behaviour they indulge in, what kind of conversations they have? I urge upon respectable families to come together and arrange an educational system for their daughters that is patterned on traditional lines. No one from a respectable family can dream of educating his daughter to work in telegraph offices or the post office."

Also see Aziz Ahmad's *Islamic Modernism in India and Pakistan, 1857-1964.* (Oxford University Press, 1967). Aziz Ahmad also sheds light on Sir Syed's basically traditional views on the question of women's education.

[10] M. Ali, *Tareekh aur Agahi.* (Lahore: Nigarshaat,1986).

[11] M. Ali, *Tareekh kay Badaltay Nazriat* (Lahore: Rohtas Publishers, 1991).

[12] Text of the official Shariat Bill, point 12.

Ideology, the BJP, and the teaching of science

Anita Rampal

Introduction

Questions of ideology shaping the school curriculum have arisen in India mostly in the context of history teaching rather than in the natural sciences. However, there have been various efforts in Europe during the last decade to radically change science teaching by exposing the implicit racist ideology of traditional curricula, which look at issues of food, population, health, disease, enviornmental decay, and so on from a perspective clearly biased against the Third World. What has also been questioned is the positivist image of science presented through textbooks, creating a mystique around its absolute authority in terms of how to view and understand the world around us. New courses have been developed that are less alienating, impersonal or sanitised, offering instead interactions that are more rooted in science and society.

With the growing stress on Science for All, science educationists the world over have become more sensitive to problems related to students' initiation into and acceptance of the subject. Science has traditionally been perceived as difficult, abstract, male-oriented and "meant only for the smartest". Its image of dealing only with "objective truths" (which often go against the grain of common sense or intuitive knowledge) has further distanced it, posing it in contradiction to other world-views in poetry, art or even religion. Restructuring the curriculum on more sound philosophical, sociological and ideological lines is currently being attempted in many countries; however, in developing countries, the challenge still remains one of evolving progressive science courses that creatively address the language, beliefs and indigenous knowledge of their diverse cultures.

Science teaching in India has remained free from overtly chauvinistic or religious controversies, unlike, for example, the prolonged "creationism vs. evolution" debate in the U.S., where some Christian scientists had lent active support to the creationists' lobby, or the more recent fundamentalist assertion of an "Islamic" science in Pakistan. The post-Independence determination to promote a "scientific temper", reiterated both by eminent scientists as well as policy makers, effectively insulated the science curriculum from possible assaults by religious bigots. Science was sufficiently idolised by the Nehruvian doctrine on development and modernity, and is still popularly believed to be the panacea for India's backwardness. In such a climate, any move to contradict established scientific theories on the basis of religious scriptures would have proved to be a self-defeating task. However, the current wave of Hindu bigotry has now conveniently chosen to co-opt modern science, unabashedly attributing the latest scientific knowledge to ancient wisdom. Attempts have also been made to undermine progressive experiments in education in favour of an authoritarian pedagogy that allows no space for the spirit of free enquiry.

In this essay I shall give an account of a progressive science teaching programme run over the last 20 years in over 500 government schools in Madhya Pradesh, and discuss the nature of the opposition it faced during the two year rule of a right-wing political party with its own educational designs.

The Hoshangabad Science Teaching Programme (HSTP)

For over two decades now the HSTP has been used in 500 government schools, spread over thirteen districts in the south-western part of Madhya Pradesh, and has been hailed as a major innovation in science education in India. The programme was initiated by field-based groups in close collaboration with a large number of scientists working in highly regarded research and teaching institutions who have continued to serve as vol ntary resource persons. It expanded radually through the administration f the state department of education, hough the academic responsibility is till borne by Eklavya, a voluntary roup funded by the central government. The focus of HSTP has been on leveloping an enquiry -oriented curiculum in which children engage in ctivities and learn mostly through he experiments they themselves perorm, rather than from lectures delivred by teachers.

One major change that necessarily ccompanied the new method of "enquiry" learning was in the examinaion system, which was radically nodified to match the emphasis on understanding, observation and experimentation, rather than on rote. An open-book system, even for the Class 8 Board examination, still continues; the framing of question papers and their subsequent evaluation is carried out collectively by teachers themselves, during special workshops held for the purpose.

Demystifying science

The mystique of science was consciously avoided in HSTP; it deliberately moved away from the highly abstract and decontextualised content of the science curriculum, which still forces boring formulae, tongue-twisting definitions and ridiculously formal formulations down the throats of young school children. Moreover, those who study in the vernacular

suffer the additional burden of the scientific discourse in "sanskritised" Hindi (or any other regional language). In the absence of a more naturally evolved and acceptable lexicon in the vernacular, the "standard" science vocabulary in such textbooks is incomprehensible even to teachers. HSTP text materials, on the other hand, attempted a more colloquial register for science, using simple everyday words wherever possible, dispensing with unnecessary technical terms which impart a formidable flavour to an already overly "scientistic" discourse.

The emphasis on the use of lowcost equipment and indigenously designed apparatus made from locally available materials, wherever possible, provided an incentive to teachers to exercise their own creative skills. Pedagogically, it was important for students to feel comfortable and familiar with the apparatus, significantly reducing the alienation and mystification normally associated with science lessons.

Children's response

The most unreserved response to the changed climate of the classroom came from children who thoroughly enjoyed the games, activities and experiments designed for them. No longer were they expected to sit passively listening to uninterrupted, boring lectures. They sat in groups of four (or more, where the batch was larger) and actively engaged with the materials or apparatus. Indeed the science classrooms became conspicuously animated and noisier, in almost cathartic defiance of the traditional strict norms of "pin-drop" silence.

Girls seem to have responded more readily to the changed curriculum and have generally shown greater maturity and responsibility in handling delicate equipment. In text materials girls were made more positively visible, and teachers as well as resource persons have become conscious of the more obvious forms of gender-bias that find their way into the science classroom. Clearly, the changed role from passive receiver to active participant — one who is expected to discuss and perform in groups, talk freely to the teacher, maintain the kit materials, collect and organise things at home or outside the classroom — has helped tremendously in building the self-confidence of girls. In fact, actice and curious girls who have learnt to question are often told at home that these science lessons have made them "too smart".

Critics of criticality

It is natural to expect some amount of resistance to any radical change from those who wish to see the status quo maintained. This programme too, has had its share of criticsism from various quarters: from the reluctant teacher-trainee who does not want to lift a finger to perform an experiment,

SARASWATI
~~INDUS VALLEY~~
CIVILISATION
42,500
~~2,500 B.C.~~
HINDU
~~PAKI~~STAN

to the piqued legislator who may fee threatened by over-confident teach ers.

Political criticism first surfaced in response to the attitude of criticality that HSTP fostered, both in its chil dren and teachers, and to the demo cratic norms it advocated. In a highly feudal state like Madhya Pradesh when teachers start asking questions and resist being harassed by petty officials of the state bureaucracy, po litical muscles promptly begin to twitch. One aggrieved legislator went to the extent of proposing in the Vidhan Sabha (Legislative Assembly) that the programme be discontinued because it was teaching children how to gamble! He said that since HSTP was based on learning by doing, it must include gambling in its new chapter on probability, where such problems were routinely discussed. What he failed to acknowledge, and

> " *It is not only a question of 30,000 mosques and mazaars. All vestiges of Mughal imperialism — whether the name of a city, village, road, building, anything that represents the barbarism of Mughal imperialism — should be removed from this country* "
>
> Swami Muktanand Saraswati, a top leader of the VHP-affiliated All India Sant Samiti

what some teachers then stood up to defend, was that the same probability problems were consciously used by them to demonstrate to children that gambling was indeed a losing proposition.

The right-wing campaign

A sustained campaign against HSTP, however, only began after the BJP government took over in the state and revealed that it had its own, very different, agenda for education. It first tried to spread the word that HSTP embodied "western science" and must therefore be discontinued. It also attempted to mobilise a campaign through its teacher organisations to show that the public was "dissatisfied" with the programme. To do this it collected various aggrieved elements from among the teachers and parents and, by highlighting people's general dissatisfacation with the deteriorating educational system in general, made HSTP a convenient target of the attack. Other curricula were considered "regular", this one the "exception", because it ran in only a small proportion of the 15,000 middle schools in the state.

A proposal recommended and supported financially by the central government for the phased expansion of such a science programme covering the entire state, was awaiting clearance by the chief minister. The BJP government made it clear that it was not going to allow such progressive voices to emerge all over the state; it shelved the proposal and threatened to terminate the existing programme. It also lost no time in expanding and strengthening its own school network (of the Saraswati Shishu Mandirs) under the umbrella organisation, Vidya Bharati. Large areas of land were allotted almost free, grants were finalised and permission given to conduct its own examinations, independent of the state boards of education.

Right-wing cadres had on occasion attempted to accuse HSTP's science activists as being "ani-national", a term they routinely used for all other activists in the state working on women, literacy, human rights, etc., who refused to join in their Hindutva mobilisation. In actual fact, most of its admirers have acknowledged that

HSTP is more rooted in the social reality of India and more concerned about reaching out to the rural majority than any other science curriculum in the country. A consistently equitable and democratic culture is nurtured, and teachers and administrators alike have been inspired by the idealism and nationalism of most resource persons, especially those prominent scientists who have voluntarily spent much time and effort in working for HSTP.

Ostensibly, the programme shared the values of idealism and nationalism that the right-wing educational agenda claimed to uphold. However, their paths diverged when it came to promoting a spirit of free enquiry, based on empirical observation and careful analysis. A democratic culture is not what right-wing education has stood for, having assiduously nurtured total subservience to authority and maintained rigid norms of discipline. Moreover, religious fundamentalists have always thrived on dictating "incontestable truths" and have conveniently mobilised people on blind faith. Inculcating a "scientific temper" is seen to be an obstacle to their specific purposes and, when required, science itself is portrayed as being "anti-religion".

Science vs religion?

Many among the HSTP teachers and resource persons have traditionally been religious and continue to follow their personal faiths without any inherent conflict. Science was seen as a specific system of knowledge based on empirical validation which did not have to interfere with one's personal philosophy or mode of worship. Such issues were discussed openly, not brushed aside uncomfortably, and often teachers were curious about the conceptions of god held by famous scientists like Einstein or Raman. Interestingly, scientists are popularly believed not to be religious in the manifest sense of the term, but "worshippers of nature", where such humility before a more "sublime force" is taken to be a natural substitute for ritualistic faith. Philosophical questions of agnosticism, or even about recognising the limitations of scientific knowledge were also debated whenever possible, for many of us are aware that, too often, science can itself take the position of an uncontested faith.

Loosening of 'closed' systems

It is true that in the Indian context it may be difficult to clearly distinguish between religious, magical or traditional beliefs, which occupy complementary domains in the space of social cognition, for unlike the West, there has been no internal confrontation between them. These beliefs, however, all fall within the category of what Horton has called a "closed" system of thought, characterised by "no developed awareness of alternatives to the established body of theoretical tenets", and therefore with no possible means available to question those tenets. Anthropologists studying traditional patterns of knowledge have highlighted the intellectual ingenuity and experimental keenness of such systems which, nevertheless, are terribly constrained by their ability to reason "within the limited idiom of their beliefs". Moving towards a scientific way of thinking would therefore involve developing an awareness of possible alternatives, so that traditional tenets become less sacred as they begin to lose their absolute validity.

On the other hand, the demarcation between science and traditional knowledge is not as sharply perceived in India. For instance, indigenous systems of medicine such as Ayurveda, Unani or homeopathy, that have had an empirico-rational basis, as distinct from other prevalent "folk" systems founded on more magico-religious practices, are popularly regarded as "scientific", contrary to the defined norms of professional science. Other examples abound.

The HSTP has stood for informed criticality in trying to understand science, its limitations and its distinction frm non-science. It has revealed the possibility of stimulating people to ask valid questions and to actively look for alternative explanations. It has tried to see the method of science as accessible to all, rather than as belonging to a body of unquestionable "expert" knowledge. It has also en-couraged a better understanding and appreciation of traditional empirical systems of knowledge possessed by farmers, artisans or housewives, and has even tried to analyse the earliest elements of scientific practice in prehistoric or even present day tribal societies. However, it has attempted to tread this path cautiously, being aware of the problems inherent in both positions. At one end are the "anti-science" propagandists, at the other are the chauvinists, only too keen to eulogise past achievements of Indian science, dangerously ready to create their own myths in the process of glorification.

Myths about ancient science

After the BJP came to power in the four states of the Hindi heartland it made a concerted effort to rewrite all school textbooks along its own ideological lines. A massive conference was held in Bhopal in which almost five thousand members of the BJP-RSS cadres participated, besides senior party leaders and the chief ministers of the four states. It was then decided to initiate major curriculum revision and to strengthen the school education programmes through the aegis of Vidya Bharati, a front organisation of the party, which was subsequently also empowered to conduct the Class 8 board examinations in M.P. (this permission however was revoked after central rule was imposed in the state in December 1992).

No Hindutva science textbooks have been printed to date, yet, typical of the BJP strategy of thriving on such publicity, much noise has been made in this regard. Any proposal to "highlight the scientific achievements of our ancient civilisation" would ormally be restricted to the history of science, which can at best be peripheral to the actual subject curriculum. However, what can be more damaging (and there have been misguided claims to this effect) would be to try to "purge" the content of its so-called " western bias" by falsely attributing modern theories to ancient knowledge. Fritjof Capra and others may have made interesting reading by merely suggesting exotic parallels betweeen quantum physics and eastern mysticism, but misguided chauvinists have conveniently co-opted this argument in their own mission of indigenous myth-making.

In Madhya Pradesh, a systematic campaign to create myths around ancient scientific achievements was conducted through various governmental and public fora, through a compulsory "foundation course" textbook for all college students, by means of frequent newspaper articles, campaigns through teachers' unions, and regular speeches by senior academics placed in responsible positions (including the chairperson of the state University Grants Commission). The local print media, unfortunately sub-servient to state power and itself too prone to sensationalise issues, was used repeatedly to reinforce this myth. The apparently appealing terms "Vedic science", "Vedic mathematics" and "Vedic economics" were thus consciously introduced into public discourse and, in conformity with well-nown fascist designs, appeared to offset somewhat a faltering national self-image.

"Vedic" mathematics is really a misnomer introduced by the BJP government in U.P. to publicise its "nationalised" high-school math textbooks, and is borrowed from a book by that title, written by Swami Bharati Krishna Tirtha of Govardhan Peeth, who proposed a system of rules for "high speed computations" based on 16 sutras, which he claimed to have derived from the Atharvaveda. These rules are only basic algorithms, or special cases of simple algebraic formulae (of the type $(a+b)(a+c) = a(a+b+c)+bc$) which, if memorised, allow for fast multiplication, division, etc. of numbers. Such rules, similar to numerous other shorthand computational methods, cannot be called a "system" of mathematics, inasmuch as they do not show how the system works. To understand that a student would need to refer back to basic algebra, which in any case is taught in every school mathematics course.

However, the BJP sought much publicity on the issue, conveniently cashing in on the term which is neither vedic or mathematics. Moreover, these math books contain patently incorrect information about different historical contributions to the discipline. The National Council for Educational Resources and Training has subsequently reviewed them and the National Steering Committee has presented a report to the Government of India recommending the withdrawal of the books. The report categorically states that the textbooks "not only present false notions on the history of mathematics and India's contribution to this basic branch of knowledge, but would also promote obscurantist notions of Indian culture and civilisatiion which would be destructive for the growth of science in India" (Recommendations of the National Steering Committee of Textbook Evaluation, 1993.)

Towards an unfettered pedagogy

The central ministry of education recently called for serious consideration of possible ways to monitor schoold textbooks, against blatant ideological distortions or even covert subversion of national policies. Education is a state subject and diverse initiatives in curriculum development are important to sustain; there is clearly need for an assertive collective community of educationists as well as an aware general public for such a monitoring exercise to be useful.

Ideological simplifications have continued to haunt our school curricula on various counts. From crude glorifications to subtler legitimations of the status quo, different ideological thrusts have invariably found their way into educational fare. Even what passes for "good" ideology often gets presented as crude idealisation, heavy moralising or tightly "encapsulated" adult positions that do not provoke children to think for themselves and cannot therefore make sense to them.

What is therefore seriously called for is to work consistently towards a truly open pedagogy, unfettered by the kind of authoritative mystifications, blatant glorifications or simplistic moralisations that normally continue to characterise all school teaching in the name of both "good" and "bad" ideology.

References

F. Capra, *The Tao of Physics* (New York: Bantam Books,1976).

E.E. Evans-Pritchard, *Witchcraft, Oracles and Magic among the Azande* (Oxford: Oxford University Press, 1936).

D. Hodson, "Social Control as a Factor in Science Curriculum Change", *International Journal of Science and Education*, Nov:9, 1987.

R. Horton, "African Traditional Thought and Western Science" in B. Wilson (ed), *Rationality* (Oxford: Blackwell, 1970).

K. Mukund, "The Hoshangabad Science Teaching Programme", *Economic & Political Weekly*, Oct. 15, 1988.

R. Pailwal & C.N. Subramaniam, "Ideology

and Pedagogy", *Seminar*, Dec. 1992.

A. Rampal, "The `Folklore' of Science and Scientists: A Case Study of School Teachers' Perceptions", Occasional Papers on Perspectives in Indian Development, Nehru Memorial Museum & Library, No.XXVI,1991

A. Rampal, "A Possible `Orality' for Science?" *Interchange*, 23(3), 1992.

A. Rampal, " `Curse' of the Green Leaves Lifted", *Times of India*, April 2,1992.

A. Rampal, "Innovative Science Teaching in India: Enabling Children to Question Societal Beliefs and Superstitions", in J. Solomon & G. Aikenhead (eds.), *Science, Technology and Society Education* (forthcoming).

W. Shukla, "Vedic Mathematics", *Seminar*, Dec. 1992.

Religion, secularism, and organising women workers

Mirai Chatterjee

Organising self-employed women around economic issues has been our main focus for several years now. In the course of our work, we have recognized and accepted the important role religion plays in women's lives, but have been more concerned with their struggles for social and economic justice. However, with the rise of communalism, and its distorted interpretations of religion, we are facing serious challenges to our work. Not only are self-employed women's economic gains being threatened, but also our very survival as a union of poor women, regardless of caste, creed or religion, is at stake. This has prompted us to further analyse and understand the role of religion in women's lives, particularly in the context of rising communalism.

Our day-to-day experience of working with poor women has led us to appreciate and respect the part religion plays in their lives. Whatever it be, our members draw tremendous strength and inspiration from their faith, the strength they need to continue to struggle both at home and at work. For even those who have begun to believe in themselves and the importance of collective action, religion remains integral. Thus, along with union meetings, discussions of women's rights and action programmes, visits to local shrines are important items on women's agendas.

Religious rituals and festivals are also of special importance to women. Preparations for these are often expensive, elaborate and time-consuming. In addition to being an expression of deep-rooted faith, they often serve as a creative outlet and a source of much enjoyment and entertainment. Whatever it is — the painting of delicate henna patterns on hands and feet at Id, or *garbas* performed with gusto at Navaratri — women are very much involved.

At the same time, increasing consciousness of the injustices they face has led SEWA members to question some aspects of religion, religious practice and the role of male clergy in all faiths. For example, at a recent discussion on religion and the commonalities between all faiths SEWA staff and members spoke of how religious women and prophets have barely been mentioned through the ages. Further, they concluded that

Karen Haydock

since historically men have controlled the writing and interpretation of religious texts, women's contribution has always been excluded.

At other times, anti-women practices in the guise of religious beliefs have been openly challenged. Several Muslim women members of SEWA have formed an imdependent support group, Mahila Talak Pidit Sangh. Apart from assisting divorced women to work and earn, the Sangh has taken up the issue of maintenance, child custody and adoption for divorced

Muslim women. Members have been supporting efforts to obtain rights for Muslim women and thus have registered their disapproval of the Muslim Women's Bill of 1986. Working within the framework of Islam and the Koran, members have been attempting to offer a new interpretation of the scriptures which hitherto have been used to justify the denial of rights to women.

Members strongly protested against the sati in Deorala village of Rajasthan in 1987. Fifty SEWA organisers went to join in a silent procession of protest in Jaipur. In addition SEWA sent a telegram and letters of protest to the Prime Minister and other senior government officials, expressing our outrage and distress at this incident. Finally, participants in a SEWA meeting of over 2000 members condemned the tragic death of Roop Kanwar.

At the community level, too, as part of our on-going activities, we have challenged unjust attitudes and behaviour towards women, passed off as "religious traditions". A few years ago, one of our members, Kamuben, was being hounded and harassed as she was said to be possessed by "evil spirits". She was weeping excessively, suffering from insomnia and according to her neighbours, "ranting and raving". Consequently, she was kept virtually without food and water in a small, unventilated room and was subjected to regular beatings by her family to get rid of the spirits and thus appease the Mother Goddess. Meanwhile, all her neighbours, including many women, taunted and abused her.

In fact, Kamuben was severely depressed as she had been recently divorced and, in an unfair but characteristic judgement, the Council of Elders had awarded child custody (including custody of a breastfeeding infant) to the husband. Despite Kamuben's desperate pleas and general consensus about the unjust deci-sion, the children were taken away. Grief-stricken Kamu's reactions led people to think she was possessed.

As SEWA has been organising women in Kamu's area around both health and economic issues, we were able to intervene in her favour. Together with our health workers, we released Kamu from the room, convinced her to eat and helped her to get some medical attention. We also discussed with people, especially women, the real reasons for Kamu's "aberrant behaviour", which was an understandable consequence of her grief and the injustice of the exclusively male Council of Elders. We found quite a positive response to our intervention, including suggestions from women that we "infiltrate" the Council.

This is but one anecdote of many such in SEWA's experience; however, action challenging religious practices can only be taken where we have a strong base of constructive activities like the union, co-operatives, health and child care, and a large membership.

Further, in terms of our goal of organising self-employed women, attacking or debunking religion in toto would have had disastrous consequences, given its importance in women's lives. Instead, at SEWA we accept and respect the role of religion and faith in our society and have stressed the humanistic aspects and commonalities between faiths. Finally, we have tried to inculcate the idea of "Sarvadharm", of the peaceful co-existence of all religious currents among us.

Having accepted the role of religion in women's lives, we are faced with an increasingly difficult situation. With the current rise of communalism, all kinds of reactionary beliefs are being peddled in the name of religion. What are these beliefs? How does communalism affect poor women? And how do we chart our course ahead?

One thing that is immediately obvious is the blatant misuse of religion by communalists. Playing on people's faith and through a narrow, selective interpretation of religious texts, communalists have already created enough havoc. There are so many examples of the misery that their dangerous rhetoric and activities have caused.[1] in 1986, during Janmashtami celebrations, Shambhu Maharaj of the Hindu Suraksha Samiti urged Hindus to take to the streets in protest as the government prevented his proposed procession.

"Babas sent by Shambhu Maharaj came to our area", said Lilaben Arjanbhai, who lives opposite the Maharaja's ashram and sews old cement bags for a living. "They said Lord Krishna has been insulted and as Hindus, we should remember our dharma and take out a procession."

These irresponsible exhortations came only two months after the terrible communal violence which rocked Ahmedabad following the Rathyatra procession in 1986. The latter, like the proposed Janmashtami procession, always winds its way through the crowded, communally tense neighbourhoods of the old city with disastrous consequences.

Today the situation has, if anything, worsened. Sadhus, mullahs and other religious leaders are making fiery speeches against one or the other community. Far from spreading love and peace between all, these self-styled leaders are spreading fear and hatred among people who once lived together in mohallas and chaals across the country.

Rhetoric and misuse of religious sentiments aside, communalism is yet another negative force in poor women's already difficult lives. Several accounts of this impact have already appeared.[2] For those lucky enough to survive communal violence, there is the loss of their homes, tools of trade, small business and valuable daily wages. Long periods of violence take a tremendous toll on the economic well-being of the city, and poor, self-employed women workers are the worst hit. For one thing, there is no question of selling vegetables and fruits from baskets in markets, or of pulling handcarts or rolling bidis. With curfew everywhere, women neither reach their workplaces nor deliver finished products made at home - bidis, readymade garments, incense sticks and other articles - to the merchants. In addition, there is no way of receiving fresh supplies of raw materials.

Sometimes, with great difficulty and considerable risk, workers manage to deliver finished goods to their employers but later, when curfew is lifted and normalcy restored, they are told by the merchants that all

Karen Haydock

records of goods received and even the goods themselves were destroyed in the violence, so how can they possibly be paid?

Further, in some areas which suffer regularly during communal violence, merchants, contractors and others refuse to give women any work. In 1985, 1986 and 1991 our area was constantly under curfew. "Our homes and few belongings were reduced to ashes. I am a readymade garment worker and have been sewing for Kanubhai of Revdi Bazaar for ten years. Now he says he simply will not give me any work. It is too much of a risk as the cloth he gave me for sewing got burned with my house and sewing machine. None of the readymade garment merchants are giving us work here. How should we eat?" asks Mehmooda, a resident of Bapunagar, Ahmedabad, and an active member of SEWA.

In addition to the loss of daily wages, both during and after the communal violence, many self-employed women lose their tools of trade, as mentioned earlier. Sewing machines, pushcarts, charkhas and small stocks of raw material and finished goods are either looted or burnt to a cinder, as explained by Mehmooda.

In 1985, SEWA restored members' tools, only to find that many of them were again destroyed in the violence of 1986 and 1990. In November 1991, when we surveyed the violence-torn areas to assess the damage suffered by SEWA members, we were pained to see the same grief-stricken faces we had encountered in 1985 and 1986. Further, burned or smashed *laris* and sewing machines which had been distributed as a relief measure in 1985 and 1986 lay abandoned outside many homes. This year too, as before, even though the government announced compensation for destroyed goods, many self-employed women could not avail of this because of lack of "proof", a prerequisite for compensation from the government. On some of the destroyed *laris* and sewing machines, the small, metallic SEWA label was still visible and some families were desperately trying to save these as "proof" for the government authorities, "When we buy a fresh stock of vegetables then abandon them and run for our lives, only to return a week later, how can we show any proof?" asked Laxmiben Patni, a vegetable vendor of Ahmedabad's Manek Chowk. Others manage to salvage bills and licences and obtain written testimony from neighbours and wholesalers. However, they still do not manage to obtain any compensation.

"I had two *laris* and had just bought four hundred litres of kerosene. When the mob came and demanded that we hand over our kerosene, we resisted for a while but what could we do? Now not only am I being told by the officers that I had no *lari* but I am also being accused of providing kerosene or arsonists," explains Valaben, a kerosene-vendor who made several fruitless attempts to obtain some compensation after the 1986 communal violence in Ahmedabad.

In the case of home- based workers, if any finished goods or raw material are destroyed, they have to bear the cost. To receive government compensation for destroyed goods, they need written documentation from their employers who, at the best of times, refuse to furnish any kind of identification cards or documents to workers. Thus we find that with repeated bouts of communal violence in an already depressed economic scene, home-based workers and other self-employed women are forced deeper into the vicious cycle of indebtedness, further pauperisation and marginalisation.

Bapunagar, Saraspur and Gomtipur are working-class neighbourhoods in Ahmedabad where thousands of home-based workers live and work. In the communal violence of 1990 these workers, among the poorest of all self-employed women, suffered terrible losses. Many of them were riot victims in 1985 and 1986, and in 1990, too, they were not spared. SEWA's estimates are that about 2200 families in these areas suffered major losses to their homes and means of livelihood, let alone loss of life. We estimate that not counting the loss of daily wages due to curfew, the material losses were not less than Rs.45 crores.

Communalism also has a divisive effect on women's unity. At SEWA we emphasise the commonalities of our experiences and struggles, bringing women of all religious affiliations under one roof. But communal violence which brings bitterness and mistrust in its wake works towards unravelling our efforts. Women who were marching through the streets together, demanding justice for all, are suddenly segregated in refugee camps. It would be impossible, under such circumstances, to expect women to be impervious to the atmosphere of fear, mistrust and divisiveness. "Sometimes we managed to keep our men indoors and sometimes we just could not," explained Hanifa, a block-printer and member of SEWA. "When the tension runs high it is difficult to stop anyone, the madness takes over. Who listens to us then?"

In the atmosphere of mistrust and despair all that keeps SEWA members hopeful and together is the knowledge that we are not alone. Although our unity is seriously challenged by the communal divide, years of struggling and sharing our everyday joys and sorrows are not so easy to erase. "In the midst of the violence, we met our Muslim sisters and brothers in Sarkhej," explained Chandaben Pappubhai, an old clothes vendor, SEWA stalwart and expert orator. "As I told all the people at the joint meeting of the city's trade unions, it is always the poor and self-employed of

Karen Haydo

all communities who suffer the most. And self-employed women are the worst affected, being the poorest of workers. There are people in this city who want to divide us, to keep us down. But we will fight back together."

What women like Chandaben have also begun to understand is that the same forces who spread the commu-nal poison also disseminate viciou anti-women propaganda. Not lon after the communal violence of 198 Hindu communalists distributed booklet expounding "Satyavad" "Theory of Truth". In this they ac vocated that women return to th home and give up their jobs in favou of "unemployed men"! To do othe wise would be to be "a witch, a falle

oman and an insult to woman-
ood".3

"You have always told us to be
rong and united," shouted Zarina, a
ormally shy and soft-spoken ready–
ade garments worker. "Where is
our unity now? We struggle the
hole year, come for meetings which
ress unity and peace, and yet we
d up as `guests' of these refugee
mps every year." Similar sentiments
ere expressed by Narmadaben, a
di worker in a refugee camp for
indu residents not far from Zarina's
mp. For SEWA and its 30,000 mem-
rs who have grown to believe that
ere will be a better tomorrow, such
riods of communal violence are
nes of reckoning.

"We worry about each other, our
milies and how to remain strong
d united. It is not easy. Many of us
ho try to preserve our linkages as
omen workers are chided, taunted
d isolated. 'Whose side are you on?'
ey ask, goading and provoking us.
hen trouble broke out at Raikhad,
me of us tried to form a women's
mmittee of both communities to
ork for peace. My husband thought
was a good idea but my relatives
dn't. Still, I kept meeting with the
er women, and our peace com-
ttee did manage to ease some ten-
n. We women understand. It is
who have to bear the brunt of
s madness," said Niruben, a SEWA
ganiser. Not all of Raikhad's resi-
nts were supportive of Niruben's

efforts, however. Her neighbours for-
bade their children to play with her's
and even rudely pushed Niruben
around in the morning queue for
milk.

Many SEWA members, like
Niruben, tried hard to maintain links
and communication even during the
worst communal violence of 1985 and
1986. In several neighbourhoods
where SEWA members of both communities live, as in Raikhad, they
worked to form peace committees and
to stifle dangerous rumours. They also
tried to keep their menfolk indoors.

Similarly, Muslim women who are
a part of the Talak Pidit Sangh
recognise that the same community
"leaders" who urge them to defend
Islam and shun other communities,
strenuously worked to prevent
women from attaining their basic
rights.

"It is these same people who oppose our coming out of our homes
and our right to maintenance and child
custody. Where are they now? Are
they helping Khairunissa,
Husnabanu, Zarina and all the others
who have been left by their husbands
to fend for themselves?" asks Rahima,
a SEWA organiser and secretary of
the Sangh.

The rising communal wave, its exploitation of religious feelings and allegiances and its destructive impact,
as we have seen above, only under-
score the need to examine our views
on religion and secularism. We need

to develop a new understanding of these from a feminist perspective. As this trend threatens our efforts for justice and equality, it is up to us to search for alternatives. Further, we will have to take the leadership in initiating actions for peace and justice for all.

To this end, we need to discuss and share our experiences, both positive and negative, with regard to religion and secularism. From this exchange ideas for action and further organising could develop, together with a strengthening of our own bonds. I would like to share some ideas for discusstion and future action.

1. We need to intensify our efforts in organising ourselves and continuing our constructive action for social and economic justice for women. This is easy to profess but harder, as we all know only too well, to translate into action and results. However, only if we have made some gains in organising and developing a support base will we be able to confront anti-women religious traditions and communal forces.

The question is, how can we build this base? Although this is not the place to go into methods of organising, it might be useful to just mention SEWA's experience. We have found that unity is built when a group of women begin to collectively perceive a common need or interest. For example, organising bidi workers, regardless of caste or religion, but around the issue of bonus or identity cards slowly creates unity among them. Common bonds forged thus are then not so easily broken even in the face of great provocation.

Another example is that of our community health centre in Bapunagar in the heart of one of the most communally tense areas. For the past three years four community health workers have been valiantly providing low cost and accessible preventive and curative health care to SEWA members. These health workers, both Hindu and Muslim, and representing bidi, agarbatti and readymade garments workers have been working together as a strong team under tremendous odds. All four of them visit all mohallas where SEWA members live, regardless of who belongs to which community.

Because all four are respected and everyone finds the health centre useful, we saw that even in the worst violence of 1990, the centre remained intact. Similarly, while the team was temporarily separated as its members were in separate refugee camps, they continued to remain in close touch with each other and even provided medical relief in the camps. Further, within a month they re-opened the health centre, resolving to work together at all costs.

2. We need to honestly recongnise that the communal virus is within all of us and in our own neighbourhoods. It is not "out there", articulated by

some fanatics. Many of us are full of communal prejudices, the result of years of socialisation and even ignorance. Thus we need to start organising against communalism from our very neighbourhoods, be they middle class or working class.

3. We need to identify and emphasise the positive, humanistic and pluralistic content of all religions. The commonalities in our religious traditions and origins need to be explored from a feminist perspective. Further, new interpretations and challenges to traditional, patriarchal religious institutions need to be undertaken.

In addition it would be important to identify the contributions to religion by women and those of religious women to society. In this attempt at a fresh analysis academics and scholars are indeed important, but there is also much to be learned from women, their folklore, rituals and songs. Next, we need to develop a clearer perspective on the little understood but much abused concept of secularism.

Along with examining our views on secularism we should actively emphasise the difference between our kind of religion and faith and that of communalism. Communalists are spending thousands on propaganda and literature, exhorting us to "return to the fold" and rediscover our religion. However, their idea of religion is patriarchal, monolithic and intolerant. We have to dissociate ourselves from this definition of "religion"; we need to build a new kind of religion, a new theology based on peace and justice for all. Liberation theologists of Latin America and elsewhere have shown that not only is a new and more relevant theology possible, but that people, particularly the downtrodden, respond in significant numbers.

As part of our organising, we should support secular movements for a common civil code. The latter, in turn, will have to be scrutinised by feminists for its approach to our problems as well as for loopholes. Further, we must protect the movement for a common code from cooption by communalists. To this end, we will have to make our voices heard through the media, in organising, and on the streets. With respect to reform or changes in personal Laws, it is not only important for all of us to join hands, but to encourage minority women to assume leadership.

Apart from our contribution to a secular civil code we should ensure that no supposedly secular policies, plans and laws discriminate against women, religious groups, dalits and the poor. To some extent, women did organise around the Muslim Women's Bill in 1986, but we were overshadowed by more powerful, vocal and organised groups. It was a sobering experience but we have to continue our efforts.

If the number of articles, papers

and discussions are any indication, feminists are increasingly concerned about the role of religion, communalism and secularism in women's struggles. We still have much to learn and understand about the part played by them in organising work, particularly at the grassroots level. Further, by exploring alternatives we can try to counter the distorted and patriarchal interpretations of religion, currently gaining ground. It is up to us to take the lead, respecting the faith dimension in women's lives and the strength it gives, and yet collectively challenging religious and communal forces that continue to obstruct our movement for justice and equality.

Notes

[1] Vibhuti Patel and Sujata Gothoskar, "The Story of the Bombay Riots in the Words of Muslim Women", *Manushi*, No.29 July-August 1985; Ammu Joseph, Jyoti Punwani, Charu Shahane, Kalpana Sharma, "Impact of Ahmedabad Disturbances on Women," *Economic and Political Weekly*, October 12, 1985 "Why This Slow Murder?" a SEWA report on the effects of communal violence in Ahmedabad, *Manushi*, No.33, March-April 1986.

[2] Ibid.

[3] Chinmay Patel, "Streedharm" in *Satyavad*,p.16. Ahmedabad Bhavani printers, 1986

Striking down a Succession Act

Mary Roy

In 1983, I challenged the Travancore Christian Succession Act which decreed that when a man died intestate (without leaving a will) his widow had a mere life estate over a portion of the family property and that "the daughter shall receive a quarter of the share of a son, or Rs. 5000, whichever is less". I took the matter to court to establish a principle. I had more money than my brothers, so it wasn't for personal gain. My intention in going to the Supreme Court was to get the old Travancore law annulled. More than 30 years ago when my father died, I had been offered Rs. 5000 as my share of my father's estate which was worth a crore. I had nursed this insult in silence for I had neither the money nor the time to invest in legal proceedings then.

Moreover, no Christian lawyer would accept my brief.

Thirty years later, when I was economically independent and therefore unconcerned about "what people would say" I travelled to Delhi and found a lawyer who accepted my brief and filed a public interest litigation case in the Supreme Court.

And so, in 1985, I challenged the Travancore Christian Succession Act as violative of my Constitutional right to equality under Articles 14 and 15 of the Constitution. The Supreme Court struck down the Act in February 1986. The Church, the legislature and the press declared that, following the judgement, there would be calamities that would hurl Kerala into hellish turmoil; that a spate of litigation which could swamp the law courts, would ensue; that the affluent Christian community would face extreme economic distress; all transactions involving Syrian Christians, like the sale of property and bank security, would be held to be invalid. *The fact that this can happen only in cases where an intestate death has occurred in the family, was never brought to general notice. It was also feared that an estimated 30,000 nuns who were not given dowry and therefore wedded to the church, would now demand their share of their fathers' property.*

My brother George's reaction to the Supreme Court ruling was vehemently "anti". He refused to accept the fact that I have a share in our father's property. At first he agreed to give my sister, Molly, and my brother, John, their shares. But not Mary Roy! His latest stand is that even Molly and John cannot claim their share because he has developed the property and spent so many lakhs on it, therefore everything belongs to him. He is prepared to make a concession and to give each of them a little; but to me, "Nothing!" He has taken a Rs 40 lakh loan from the State Bank of Travancore, giving father's property as collateral security, which more than covers his and my mother's shares. She says, "Of course, I will give Mary Roy her share," but the fact is, there is no share left. She worships this brother of mine. She would, blindfolded, do whatever he wished because of her conviction that what she has suffered all these years will be washed away one day by her son. George, by the way, is a Rhodes scholar, brilliant, and a well-known intellectual. He now runs this food factory which my mother started in Kottayam.

In 1989 I filed a suit in the District Court praying that the partition of my father's property be ordered by the Court according to the Indian Succession Act. Father died in 1959, and ever since, my brother and my mother were in possession of all the property. We had no objection to mother living in the ancestral property and enjoying the income, but the partition should show who the owners of the property are, and it should not be used to raise more loans.

The District Court passed an interim order which upheld the right of my brother and mother to take more loans, using this property as collateral. I appealed against it to the High Court: the Court directed that my share of my father's property not be encumbered. My sister Molly and brother John have also petitioned the Court to safeguard their rights.

Hearings have not yet begun. It is going to be impossible to dislodge the brother who is in possession, conceding the delays involved in the legal process. It is clear that none of us are going to inherit anything in our lifetime. The battle goes on, because, as a matter of principle, I cannot withdraw.

Concerning matters of inheritance, my family is not unusual. Let me tell you about 67 year old Aleykutty (a gutsy woman if ever there was one) also involved in a similar bid to dislodge her brother who is in possession of the intestate property of their father. Aleykutty had impleaded herself in my petition in the Supreme Court in 1983. Here is her story:

We rejoiced after the 1986 Supreme Court verdict striking down the

Travancore Christian Succession Act. Now we could claim our legacy. Little did we know that we would probably never see our legacy in our lifetime.

After our father's death, our only brother turned us out of the house—mother and five sisters. We eked out a living. I was a nurse. Euphrasis, my sister, was also a nurse, and Denise the youngest sister who has polio, has a job as a teacher. Two of our sisters became nuns, for there was no way to educate them or get them married. We bought a little plot of land and built a house where all of us could live together. Then we decided to get Euphrasis married. We gave her the house we built as dowry. Her husband turned out to be an alcoholic, so that was the end of Euphrasis's marriage.

"Came the historic verdict of the Supreme court. A month after the verdict, my brother produced a will supposed to have been written in 1981 by my father... that is before we filed our case in the Supreme Court. If this will were genuine, we would have had no claim, for according to the will neither my mother nor any of us sisters were given anything by our father. So back we went to Court. The Court gave its verdict: THE WILL IS FALSE.

The end was still not in sight. Obviously, my brother, now enjoying our father's 12 acres of land would appeal against the judgement in the Kerala High Court, and then in the Supreme Court. He had the money to do this.

He was the youngest of the family, and so had time also on his side.

We knew that waiting for the Courts would mean waiting until death. I had to have a house which I could call my own. I had to get some income from my father's land. So I called together a loyal band of labourers who had known our family for years. I moved into a three - acre plot of land below the great church on the hill, which my father had built. During the course of one day we built four walls with brick. The room is about 30' by 20'. A single room, with a partition for a kitchen. The lavatory is outside. The roof is made of coconut leaves. The floor is mud with cowdung smeared over it. There is no electricity. No water. But my neighbours help me with all I need. I am all alone, so one of them comes to sleep with me at night. But it is my land. My house.

My brother brought a policeman in his car. The policeman was kind. He whispered to me to finish the work quickly. He said, "According to the Truth of God and the Truth of Man what your are doing is fine. But it is against the law."

Aleykutty and her polio-stricken sister themselves tapped the rubber from the rubber trees in the plot and got 40 sheets of rubber. At Rs. 10 per sheet, that is an income of Rs. 400. She got 15 coconuts from her trees. She and her sisters have stared cultivating a small paddy field (also belonging to their father) in spite of the fact that the brother turned out four great buffaloes into the field." We have enough paddy for the year!" says Aleykutty with a mischievous gleam in her eyes.

A brave woman! How many more are there like her? The fingers of one hand would be too many to count them!

What are the other repercussions of the Supreme Court verdict whereby women get an equal share in intestate property?

I have already given you the example of one interesting fallout: the writing of wills in order to disinherit daughters. Christians who were superstitious about writing wills are now being advised by their churches to do so in order to overcome the complications arising from the new succession act. Lawyers claim that writing wills is big business now.

Marriages continue to be arranged with huge sums of money changing hands in order to circumvent the Dowry Prohibition Act. The wedding day is an excellent occasion to get the bride and the groom to sign legal documents declaring that the bride does not have any further interest in her father's property.

The Supreme Court verdict was retrospective in nature: it applied to all intestate deaths which had occurred after 1956. This has caused understandable embarrassment; however, in most cases, a little arm-twisting solves the problem. Very often the problem is solved by the excellent relationships that prevail within families!

It has been found that due to the retrospective nature of the judgement property documents are not in order, because the daughters have had no part in the partition. Thus documents offered as collateral to banks are rejected as defective.

What is the solution? I really am not competent to answer this question. Maybe, a little "giving" and a little more "love" by both men and women would be a great solution. Maybe a government tribunal could help to settle disputes within a time-barred period of two years or so. Let me recount the odd repercussions that still plague me:

(a)   The verdict is dated February 1986. In May 1986 (three months later) my brother fired his first missile. He claims that I did not admit his daughter to my school because he would not give me a donation — black money — to be paid to me personally without receipt. Funny, that no one else in the 23 years that Corpus Christi has existed, has made similar charges ! George sits in court every single day when there is a hearing. The desire for revenge seeps through every pore in his body!

The oddest reaction of all came from the Income Tax Department. A demand that I should pay tax on my share of my father's property which I am going to inherit.

A demand for payment now !

I have been advised to give a petition to the Chairman of Direct Taxes in Delhi, and explain that:

(a) there are many Christian women like me;

(b) it is likely that in our lifetime we will not inherit

     our share of our father's property;

(c) until we do inherit, it is unlikely that women have the means to pay the tax.

Strangely enough, neither my brother nor my mother were served with similar notices!

The positive results

That women do have rights is conceded, and very often this is the subject of heated discussion.

More women are beginning to see that courts are not evil and that questioning the old patriarchal order is not a sign of rebellion.

Many fathers and brothers have included women in the partition of property, as they see the need for doing so.

Maybe women are more resistant to change than men! In the early days, a congregation of Catholic women made a representation to the Central Parliamentary Affairs Ministry to the effect that they did not want any share in their fathers' property.

On the whole, the social system is not ready for these changes and laws can do little to force such issues. Nevertheless, antiquated laws must be wiped off the statute books.

Illustrations: Amili Setalvad & Communalism Combat

लोग टूट जाते हैं
एक घर बनाने में
तुम तरस नहीं खाते
बस्तियां जलाने में
— बशीर बद्र

Rajasthan Kisan Sanghatana

Dukhtaran-e-Millat: profile of a militant, fundamentalist women's organisation

Shiraz Sidhva

The week in December that Rubaiya Sayeed, the then Home Minister's daughter, was kidnapped 1989, thousands of Kashmiris — men, women and children — took to the streets, singing, shouting slogans and setting Indian flags aflame. The women who turned out in large numbers and congregated at street corners, chanting revolutionary songs and clapping with fervour, were hardly concerned about the well-being of their kidnapped sister, as the rest of India was. They wanted the Indian government to free five militants in exchange for Rubaiya, a doctor in Srinagar. The women were especially keen that the People's League leader, Shabir Shah, be released. Loud, excited cries of "Shah, Shah Shabir Shah" rent the air for over thirty-six hours, which proved to be yet another turning point in Kashmir's troubled history.

Those were heady days, and some Kashmiris believed that azaadi, independence for their state from India, was around the corner. The Jammu and Kashmir Liberation Front's ruse to hold the minister's daughter to ransom worked. The ten-day old government of Vishwanath Pratap Singh released five militants in exchange for Mufti Mohammed Sayeed's daughter. December 1989 was the beginning of Kashmir's most violent phase, one for which there is no end in sight yet.

Over the last few years, women in Kashmir have seen their lives completely disrupted and even destroyed by militancy and the efforts of the State to repress the popular insurgency in the valley. In the early days of 1990 the women used to march in large numbers to protest against the State killings. The security forces found it tougher to hit out at the women who led most of the protest marches, shielding men from the lathis of the forces. Women have been sitting on daily dharnas in large groups at the city's jails to free the boys who had been picked up, often arbitrarily, and when the militants committed excesses, the women protested against their own boys, too.

Kashmiri women have picketted the streets of Srinagar and other towns and villages to voice their agitation about rape and killings by the security forces, and have been an important part of the well-oiled propaganda machinery of the militants. In February 1993, when two senior Hizbul Mujahideen leaders were shot in cold blood in a euphemistic "encounter" in Kralpora village, hundreds of women left their homes and marched in stunned silence down the sides of the narrow highway on the road to Srinagar. "India has gone too far, and we are prepared to fight to the last man," says Nafisa, a 23-year old woman clutching a small child. "And after the last man is dead, it will be the women who will carry on the struggle."

After the first incident of rape by security forces in Chhanpora, a Srinagar suburb, militants circulated video tapes of women telling their story about how the attack had happened. That evening, the tell-tale signs of wanton destruction by jawans were all too evident, and a group of women gave graphic descriptions of how 30 women had been raped, some of them gang-raped. But not one of the 30 women was present to testify about herself and it was not possible to trace them to the relatives' houses that their families claimed they had been evacuated to. Though it was evident that there had been violence during a search by Central Reserve Police personnel, there was less evidence to suggest the widespread attack on women being implied on the video cassettes. The Chhanpora incident was the first of such cases of women playing an active role in projecting the movement. The Kunan-Poshpora rape in February 1991 is another case in point. As time went by, the women in the small village that had obviously been traumatised by the army, became more and more strident in their description of atrocities, and the number of women who said they had been raped steadily increased. As one of the first visitors to the village three weeks after the incident (the place was snowbound and inaccessible before that) it was obvious to me that something terrible had indeed happened that night, but it was difficult to establish either its scale or extent.

For a conservative Muslim woman to publicly declare that she has been raped, pose for pictures in the newspapers and testify on camera only illustrates the degree of politicisation of Kashmiri women. Attempts to verify their stories have sometimes been frustrating. The point here is not that there have been no rapes or excesses in the valley, — there have; but that women may exaggerate the all-too bitter truth in order to gain support for the movement which had largely been ignored by the super-powers because of its projection as fundamentalist. In early 1990, some militant groups like the Allah Tigers enforced a ban on liquor shops, beauty parlours, cinema halls and video libraries. Women by and large supported the movement, and some of them felt that adhering to the tenets of Islam would only help them better their situation in an atmosphere of rapidly deteriorating social circumstances. For the first time, a dress code was prescribed for Kashmiri women, with militant groups insisting that they wear burqas and cover themselves from head to foot.

The emergence of an organised women's group was apparent in early 1990, when the Dukhtaran-e-Millat gave a call for women to march to the United Nations on March 14, the first curfew-free day after the Chhanpora rape incident. Thousands of women filled the Maulana Azad Road that leads from Lal Chowk at the city centre to Gupkar, where the UN office is situated. Hundreds of Central Reserve Police Force and Border Security Force men were marching alongside the peaceful procession of women under the Dukhtaran-e-Millat banner, to protest against the alleged rapes and wanton killings in the valley over the last two months. Suddenly, and without any obvious provocation, women were subjected to tear-gassing and lathi blows and they ran for cover, which there was very little of, onto the main road to the safety of a small mosque opposite the government tourist centre; they were locked in there when police found they could not enter. Some of the women who were sobbing uncontrollably when they emerged from the ordeal, said that it would only make them more determined to fight for azaadi.

Among the marchers that day was a short, burqa-clad girl who was busy shouting instructions to the others and pleading to them to keep calm. She introduced herself as Aasiyeh Andrabi, the leader of the Dukhtaran-e-Millat, or Daughters of the Faith.

I asked her why she and so many other women— though by no means all — were wearing burqas to the march. (Kashmiri women often cover their heads with a chaddar, but the burqa is not a common sight at all.) The dress had proved restrictive when some women tried to clamber up a low wall to the relative safety of a football field by the side of the road. "The Koran teaches us that women should always wear the burqa — unfortunately, my sisters are not disciplined, and they have fallen prey to India's anti-Muslim indoctrination and abandoned the burqa. The Koran teaches us that a woman can do anything in a burqa, even fight a war if need be, and Insha Allah, the day is not far when every Kashmiri woman will wear the burqa and live by the tenets of Islam."

Andrabi, who is widely regarded as the leader of the women's movement, was arrested in early 1993 and continues to languish in jail with her infant son. She was accused of anti-national activities by the Indian government and arrested, along with her militant husband, at Srinagar airport. Though she has been underground for much of the last three years, she seized every available opportunity to project her views on Islam and the movement to visiting journalists, and was very conscious of the international dimensions of the

देख देख देख कोई मंदिर मस्जिद बोट काट रहे हैं हम बह्ग बांट रहे हैं कोन रहे हैं सबको रहे

Kashmir problem. "You misunderstand us," she once admonished me during a discussion on whether Islamic fundamentalism protected Muslims to the exclusion of everyone else. "We are pro-Islam, not anti-Hindu, Sikh or Christian," she argued. "You boast about India being a secular nation," says Nikhat, another member of the organisation. "It is your government which is fundamentalist, it is India which is a terrorist state. Otherwise, why would the vast majority of Hindus sit silent when so many Sitas in the valley are being made to suffer the gravest humiliations?"

The Dukhtaran-e-Millat was founded in Kashmir in 1987, as the women's wing of the pro-Pakistan, fundamentalist Jamaat-e-Islami, inspired by its counterpart headed by Rabia Gilani in Azad Kashmir. Using Islam, or one interpretation of it, to help women come to terms with the militancy in the valley is the main task of this political outfit. The organisation is cadre-based at the city, district and village levels, and though it is hard to believe that 80 per cent of Kashmiri women are members of the Millat (as its office-bearers claim) there is widespread support for their activities, especially on social issues like enforcing prohibition in the valley and insisting that women forego dowry to help their fellow citizens tide over difficult times.

The Dukhtaran-e-Millat's campaign against dowry has been fairly successful, allowing the group to take luxuries like jewellery and fancy utensils and clothes from the rich, to distribute essentials, like food, among the poor. Groups of women would visit a house where a marriage was about to take place and impress upon the bride the need to sacrifice her dowry to help the larger cause. "If the woman doesn't agree of her own volition, we seize the goods by force," says Nahida Nasreen, general secretary of the party.

Besides forming an effective buffer, providing emotional and material support in times of crisis and death and the all-too frequent tragedies that most families have had to face, the Millat indoctrinates women into accepting the rigours of militancy. "We have to impress upon our sisters their role in the movement," said Aasiyeh Andrabi, months before she was arrested early in 1993. "They are the ones who have to encourage their husbands and brothers to join the jehad for azaadi. If a woman cringes and cries, the menfolk think twice about leaving their families and going out to war, but if, on the other hand, she enthuses the menfolk to fight on, they get the added moral strenth that they need to enter the battlefield."

Representing the most well-defined women's group in the valley, the Dukhtaran-e-Millat operates within a larger context of passive resistance by Kashmiri women as a whole. This role has taken different forms, ranging from shielding militants in their homes, misleading the security forces and acting as

couriers and information-gatherers. One father in Batmaloo went to the exten
of allowing a dreaded Hizbul Mujahideen militant into bed with his youn
daughter to protect him from jawans during a cordon-and-search operation i
1990. Women form a vital part of the valley's militant propaganda networ
which the Indian government's own propaganda machinery has a hard tin
keeping pace with.

In an environment of subterfuge the burqa, which has been projected as
symbol of Islam, becomes a functional necessity. Just as the woollen phira
became a dreaded garment for the security forces, with militants being able t
hide deadly weapons within its folds without being detected, so too, the burc
helped clandestine operations, often required in troubled times.

Apart from a short-lived phase in 1992 when members of the Millat threw
paint and ink on women refusing to wear the burqa, there have been no case
of coercion as far as ensuring that it is adopted. The Millat's move to forc
women into burqas was widely criticised within the valley, though the India
government gave it much publicity to illustrate the fundamentalist nature c
the struggle. The immediate resistance to a change in dress code came from th
urban educated elite, with college girls refusing to respond to such attacks an
condemning them.

Their resistance got support from Kashmiri women, especially in the rura
areas, because the burqa has never been part of traditional Kashmiri dres
Women wear a kasaba or ornate headgear, and a long phiran, their faces neve
covered. The emancipation of Kashmiri women in modern times has its roo
in "Naya Kashmir", the landmark manifesto of Sheikh Abdullah's Nation,
Conference Party, published in 1944. It was widely believed to have bee
written by Freda and BPL Bedi, a leftist couple working for the Communi,
Party of India in the valley, and the progressive tone of the document laid th
foundation for a more active role for women in social and political emancipa
tion, one that Sheikh Abdullah endorsed. The National Conference even had
full-fledged women's wing which sustained the Quit Kashmir movemer
between 1944-1946 (launched against Maharaja Hari Singh in 1931), whe
most of its leaders like the Sheikh and Mirza Afzal Beg were arrested, an
others like GM Karra and Bakshi Ghulam Mohammed were underground.

The involvement of women reached its peak in 1948 when they formed a
armed brigade to ward off Pakistani infiltrators. The slogan of the time wa
Hamlawar khabardaar, hum Kashmiri hain tayyaar (Aggressors beware, w
Kashmiris are prepared). Women played a crucial role again in the agitatio
that followed the disappearance of the Prophet's Hair from Hazratbal Shrin
in 1963. They ran community kitchens on the streets of Srinagar in the bitin

cold to help Kashmiris stay outdoors and protest until the holy relic was found. "The pride of Kashmir has been saved by the women of Kashmir," said Abdul Rahim Banday, the custodian of the relic.

There are smaller, yet significant instances of resistance by Kashmiri women. In 1967, they led an agitation demanding a ban on the Book of Knowledge, a Christian text containing a picture of the Prophet Muhammed, which is considered blasphemous. Similarly, when the Government College for Women on Residency Road, in the heart of Srinagar, was sought to be renamed after Jawaharlal Nehru, women flooded the streets in angry protest.

The level of emancipation of women in Kashmir was certainly higher than in most Islamic countries, and better than in most other Indian states. While mainstream Islam had no women saints, Kashmir's most revered one, Lalla Arifa, or Laleshwari, was a woman. Lalla Arifa, who roamed the streets of Srinagar singing her legendary verse in the early 16th century, introduced Sufism to the valley and questioned the existing social order. The Sufi saint, along with Habba Khatoon or Zooni, the queen of ruler Yusuf Shah Chak, provided the role models for Kashmiri women to actively participate in politics and social reform movements. Habba Khatoon helped her artistically inclined husband to repel frequent Mughal onslaughts on the valley, and practically ruled Kashmir.

This historically inherited social consciousness among the women of Kashmir, along with the introduction of a charter of state-sponsored women's rights in 1944, ensured their participation in political activity. The state's progressive land reforms of 1949-51, when large estates were abolished and surplus land redistributed among peasants, contributed to the economic independence of women. The occupational structure and the family-based workforce provided rural women with employment opportunities, giving them a say in politics as well. In urban Kashmir, a policy of reservations for women provided them with employment opportunities in government, though the low level of literacy made the scheme ineffectual.

Nahida Nasreen, head of the Millat since Aasiyeh's arrest, explains that her organisation's primary task is to undo the anti-Islamic propaganda that India has indulged in over the last forty years through radio and television. "Muslims are suppressed all over the world, even though they dominate the population," says the burqa-clad women's leader, a post-graduate in zoology and Arabic. "India has tried to tell us that there is no difference between Islam and other religions, when in fact Islam gives women much greater freedom and special rights. Allah created us as precious beings, and the burqa keeps us in safe custody. Purdah gives us more izzat and I am proud of it. Nowhere in

Islam will you find degrading practices like sati, and widow remarriage is not frowned upon in our religion."

Nahida dismisses Sufism as an "alien Islam", and says it will only prevent Muslims from ruling the "whole world" as they were ordained to — "Allah created us for that purpose." The Millat sees Kashmir as part of a pan-Islamic world, even though the majority of Kashmiris do not subscribe to this view. Despite its unpopularity for trying to impose purdah, the Millat enjoys mass support because it strives to fill an ideological vacuum at a time when society is seen to have degenerated. In the early 1980s, the more liberal behaviour of the ruling elite led by Chief Minister Farooq Abdullah, coupled with his economic policy encouraging tourism as the largest industry, caused visible strains in the social fabric. There was a spurt in prostitution and drug-peddling, and a very real fear that the valley would become so tourist-oriented that its population would be forced to do anything to pander to visitors.

Referring to the historic episode of the Prophet's wife, Ayesha Siddique, leading an army, the Dukhtaran-e-Millat says that Islam provides for women to pick up the gun if the need arises. "We are prepared to take to the gun, but only after there are no men left to fight," says Aasiyeh. This explains the fact that though women are involved in the militancy, there has not been a single case of an armed woman militant, even though some have reportedly been trained to use weapons. It will be a while before Kashmiri women actually wield guns and enter mainstream militancy. Until then, they will continue to be the backbone of the popular insurgency in the valley against the armed forces.

Poster: Chandralekha

"All our goddesses are armed":

religion, resistance and revenge in the life of a militant Hindu nationalist woman[1]

Paola Bacchetta

"To those of you who say you are ashamed to be Hindus, we want to tell you: we are ashamed of YOU. After December 6, the tiger has been let out of the cage "

Uma Bharati at the VHP's
Global Vision 2000
in Washington

Recent scholarship on women and right-wing movements has attempted to explain women's participation in anti-Other organisations in a range of modes. Some of the earliest literature on the subject maintained that right-wing women are simply alienated from their own interests, and their actions represent coherency with the interests of their male counterparts.[2] A second current put forth the notion that women join primarily out of a desire for community with other women who share their background, and not because they adhere to the anti-Other stance of the organisation.[3] In a third tendency, which I find the most pertinent, scholars see women's adherence as motivated by "conviction, opportunism and active choice".[4]

Here, I would like to push that last analysis one step further by exploring some of the modalities and one of the factors, the symbolic dimension, which are operational in the "active choice" made by women militants in the Hindu Nationalist context. In order to do so, I shall focus on the life of one particularly committed, dynamic member of the Rashtra Sevika Samiti (hereafter, the Samiti), named Kamlabehn.[5] I gathered the data which form the substance for analysis in interviews I conducted with her sporadically over a period of four years, from 1987 to 1990, in her hometown, Ahmedabad (Gujarat).[6]

Kamlabehn is in her 30s and her main role in the organisation is teaching paramilitary skills such as riflery, karate and lathi-wielding to other members. She is physically tough and highly confident of herself. She is an atheist, and she believes that women are as able as men, including as warriors. In many ways, Kamlabehn is not so different from most of the other young sevikas (Samiti members, meaning also "workers") whom I have met. Her age, upper caste and middle class background place her at the average of the Samiti's membership. However, I would not like to claim that she is a "typical" sevika, for there is no such thing. I have demonstrated elsewhere that the Samiti accommodates a wide range of personalities, statuses, lifestyles, modes of adherence and agential strategies and mechanisms.[7] Kamlabehn is simply among those who go the farthest in revolting against standard models for domesticated femininity and in rewriting her own identity as a fierce and fiercely independent woman. In what follows I would like to explore how she does this and why.

One of the means Kamlabehn uses to legitimise her resistance to normative femininity involves the skilful manipulation of the language of Hindu nationalism to formulate that resistance in terms that can be understood and accepted in her environment. A major point of reference in that language is hatred of the designated Others of Hindu nationalist discourse, notably "the muslims."[8] Indeed, I shall argue that Kamlabehn's

notion of the feminine Self and the space of relative freedom that she carves out for herself absolutely depend upon constructing "the muslims" as demonic, threatening, and in particular, threatening to Hindu women. I shall explore this dimension in depth, but first, a brief discussion of the Samiti and its conception of the Self is in order, since the Samiti provides much of the material which Kamlabehn uses to reformulate her own notions.

Rashtra Sevika Samiti and the Self

The Samiti is the women's wing of the paramilitary, non-party Hindu nationalist organisation, the Rashtriya Swayamsevak Sangh (hereafter, the Sangh).[9] It was established in Wardha, Maharashtra (then the Central Provinces) in 1936, eleven years after its male counterpart and in close geographical proximity to the latter's birthplace, Nagpur. Its founders were Dr. Hedgevar, the founder and first Sarsanghchalak (Supreme Leader) of the Sangh, and an ex-Gandhian activist and widowed mother of eight, Lakshmibai Kelkar. The Samiti was the first organisation of the Sangh's now-massive network known as the Sangh Parivar. The latter consists of hundreds of affiliates which mobilise various sectors of society according to their profession (in unions) or around issues (cow protection, temple "reconversion", etc.).

From its inception, the Samiti

dopted the Sangh's overall goal, its
tructure and techniques. The shared
hort-term objective of both
rganisations is to abolish the present
ecular Indian state and to impose a
Hindu Nation in its place. The Hindu
Nation would exclude non-Hindus
rom the citizenship-body (Indian
Muslims, of course, but also Parsis,
Christians, Jews, etc.) as well as a
reat many people who call them-
elves Hindu but who do not con-
orm to the Sangh's ascetic machoised

Communalism Combat

Hindu nationalist ideals. The latter
ategory includes members of certain
antrik and shakta sects, secular Hin-
us, gay Hindus and many other sec-
ors or people within Hinduism.

In conformity with the Sangh, the
amiti's structure is rigidly hierarchi-
al, with positions of power edging
ownward from the national to the
ocal levels. Similarly, its basic unit is
he shakha, or neighbourhood cell,
which meets for an hour daily or, in

some cases, weekly. Like the Sangh,
the Samiti's primary activities are the
ideological and paramilitary training
it offers to its members during shakha.
It runs extensive programmes on an
on-going basis designed to attract
middle class women (art shows, yoga
classes, etc.) or low-income women,
or both (for example, its public cel-
ebration of its self-designated national
Hindu festivals).

Today the Samiti has about one
million members who operate out of
shakhas based in at least sixteen of
India's states and several countries
abroad. The shakhas are concentrated
in areas where the Sangh is particularly active. In that sense, they reflect
the Samiti's original membership
which consisted largely of the women
relatives of the swayamsevaks (Sangh
members, literally "self-workers" or
"volunteers"). These continue to
monopolise positions of power at the
higher echelons of the organisation.
Today, however, with the reorient-
ation of the Sangh and some of its
family organisations towards populism and mass-recruitment under the
leadership of Sarsanghchalak Bala-
saheb Deoras (since 1973), the Samiti
has likewise strategically expanded
its membership downward to include
women from wider sections of society. Some of the activities it carries
out for these purposes include the
establishment of income-generating
and job-training projects in urban
slums, involvement in housing

struggles among the poor, running shelters for homeless women, organising free puja and Sanskrit classes in villages, and disseminating information on hygiene and health to the urban and rural poor. Indeed, the Samiti posits itself as an "indigenous", "authentic" alternative to Indian feminist and developmental organisations which, it maintains, come from "outside".[10]

Both the Samiti and the Sangh are intimately concerned with questions of "religious" and gender identity, and they envision them as interdependent. The investment in the notion of identity is reflected in the Sangh's name which includes the word "self"; in contrast, it is repressed as a signifier in the Samiti's name. That is, the Sangh's name means literally National (Rashtriya) Self (Swayam) Worker (Sevak) Association (Sangh). The self in question is the material self-acting-in-the world as opposed to the immaterial, spiritual self (the atman or the brahman). Indeed, in the Sangh's ideology, the realisation of the Hindu Nation depends upon the realisation of individual and collective Hindu males on the material plane. In an obvious translation of orthodox Brahmanical modalities for spiritual self-realisation to fit its material goals, the Sangh puts forth that each Hindu male is to peel back the layers of maya which are blinding him to his essential Hindu nationalist self, and this is to be done individually and collectively through seva (service) in the Sangh itself. Once enough Hindu men realise themselves in that manner, they will be able to "resurrect" the ideal Hindu Nation. In contrast to the Sangh's open statement about itself in its name, the Samiti's name means simply Nation (Rashtra) Workers (Sevika) Association (Samiti). Despite the effacement of the signifier "self", the Samiti is very engaged in constructing ideal models for powerful symbolic femininity and powerful material womanhood.

Indeed, it is in their ideal models for femininity / masculinity and women/ men that the Sangh and the Samiti diverge most sharply.[11] Briefly stated, the Sangh assigns mainly passive qualities to Hindu femininity and womanhood, while the Samiti tends to represent them more widely in terms ranging from domesticated to fierce to out-of-control. The major hidden reference for such qualities is the *Devi Mahatmya*, an ancient Sanskrit text which the Samiti draws upon but which the Sangh ignores. The characteristics designated as feminine put forth by the Samiti are reinforced in the organisation's symbolic register in the form of two goddesses: Bharatmata and Ashta Bhuja.

Bharatmata is a goddess which the Samiti inherited from the Sangh; for both organisations, she represents the territoriality of the Hindu Nation. Elsewhere i have demonstrated that he Sangh has historically attempted o curb powerful symbolic femininity by depicting her as benevolent, violated by the enemies of the Hindu Nation, raped and vivisected by "the muslims".[12] The Samiti, in contrast, adopts the signifier Bharatmata but opens up the field of representation to include even the most ferocious of qualities as her signifieds. In addition. Samiti publications refer to Bharatmata alternatively as Parvati and Durga, thereby concretising the gamut of possible interpretations and subtlely linking her to the *Devi Mahatmya*, in which the latter play key roles.

Ashta Bhuja (literally, the eight-armed goddess) in contrast, belongs solely to the Samiti. She was invented by Lakshmibai Kelkar[13] as a symbol to unify members. Later, an icon of the deity was installed at Wardha, the earliest site of the Samiti headquarters. The literature describes Ashta Bhuja as "an integral combination of Mahakali, Mahasaraswati and Mahalaxmi."[14] She represents "co-ordination of Strength, Intellect and Wealth" which "elevates the nation to a higher plane."[15] She carries "weapons in all eight hands" which "symbolise the qualities necessary for an ideal Hindu woman".[16] In her iconographic representation, she holds a saffron flag (Bhagwa Dhwaj, the Sangh-appropriated symbol of its Hindu Nation), a lotus, the Bhagavad Gita, a bell, fire, a sword, a rosary; the eighth hand is empty but posed in a blessing gesture. Finally, the Samiti suggests the mode in which members are to relate to Ashta Bhuja: each sevika "takes inspiration from her and exerts for just cause and service to humanity."[17] A Samiti prayer is offered to her at the shakhas; it refers to her as "the eight-handed goddess who rides a tiger" and specifically nominates her as "Mother Durga who slays the enemies",[18] thereby emphasising her fierce qualities and, again, suggesting a connection between her and a fierce form of the goddess in the *Devi Mahatmya*. In addition, many sevikas (but not Kamlabehn) worship her at home as their personal deity.[19] Indeed, the qualities assigned to her and the instructions on how to relate to her are sufficiently flexible to allow for their translation into practice in a heterogeneity of modes. In what follows I shall discuss Kamlabehn's subjective interpretation of these. But first, some background information on Kamlabehn, her significant Others and her context.

Kamlabehn

Kamlabehn belongs to a family of Maharashtrian Brahmins who migrated to Gujarat. She perceives herself as intimately connected to her personal ancestors but, like most Sangh and Samiti respondents I have interviewed, she places them in a wider network of relations. That is,

मौत और आतंक का यह सिलसिला कब तक?
धर्म प्रेम बढ़ाता है ख़ौफ नहीं!

आग की आँखें नहीं होतीं,
ना ही फ़र्क करती वह
शब्बर हुसैन और बुध सिंह में,
नहीं पहचानती वह
किसी राजनीति या सियासत को,
किसी धर्म या मज़हब को ।

she conceptualises herself as a link in a genealogical chain which began prior to her birth and which will continue after her death, but which is expanded to include the whole of the "Hindu people", in the past/present/future. Within this scheme, she valorises her immediate family and their Hindu nationalist activities over all. She points out that she was "a sevika from before birth", since her family has always been an "RSS family". In Hindu nationalist parlance, an RSS family is one in which elder family members of both genders, and in particular the parents, belong respectively to the Sangh and the Samiti. Kamlabehn's family certainly qualifies since both parents and all her siblings are members, although they are active in varying degrees. Of all the family members, Kamlabehn has invested the most time and energy in Hindu nationalist activities. Her parents and siblings (all of whom are married) are preoccupied with their nuclear and joint familial responsibilities. In contrast, Kamlabehn has reduced her familial responsibilities to a minimum in order to devote more time to the Samiti.

Kamlabehn's natal home is located in a middle class "all-Hindu area" of the city. The neighbourhood is largely inhabited by Maharashtrian Brahmins and RSS families. In Ahmedabad, a disproportionate percentage of local Sangh and Samiti leaders and highly active members come from such a background.

Kamlabehn's natal household was nuclear; it consisted of both parents, an elder brother, two older, and one younger, sisters. Her father worked as a government administrator who, due to the nature of his work, was often absent from Ahmedabad. Her mother was not employed, but "she managed the whole house, and gave service to the Samiti too". Kamlabehn points out that her father "was educated for a career", while her mother who is "intelligent" was "prepared for motherhood only". Kamlabehn explains this difference in their upbringing not in terms of gender but rather as due to the fact that her father's side of the family was an RSS family while her mother's was not. In this, she expresses a view common among sevikas: they see membership in an "RSS family" as liberating compared to the non-RSS context. Kamlabehn admires both parents for their active commitment to Hindu nationalism, but emphasises her mother's merits and the strength required to break with her "traditional upbringing". Her mother's rupture with her past and reconstruction of her present in Samiti terms served at least partially as a model for Kamlabehn's own dynamic process of identity reformulation albeit consistently within the context of the Samiti.

Unlike some of my respondents, but in coherence with Gananath

Obeysekere's observation on modes of self-representation among his Hindu informants,[20] Kamlabehn does not emphasise the earliest years of her life. Instead, she speaks glowingly about her most recent ones.

When Kamlabehn came of age, like her elder siblings and most of the other children in her neighbourhood, she was sent to a local English-medium school. Despite their anti-western discourse, I found it to be common practice among middle class RSS families to send their own children to such schools and later abroad for studies, if possible. Early on, Kamlabehn showed an aptitude for the natural sciences. Her father encouraged her in this domain until finally she pursued higher education in engineering. He often supported her entrance into areas traditionally confined to men.

As a child Kamlabehn's most significant young feminine Other was a schoolfriend named Gita who also belonged to an family. Both girls attended shakha: the attraction was "playing games and the stories about famous Hindu women". After matriculating Kamlabehn, who had no desire to marry, began to attend a local engineering school. She lived at home, commuted on her motorbike and was rarely accountable to her family for her time. Once, in a discussion on that period, Kamlabehn's mother complained to me that her daughter "has always gone gallivanting around as she pleases". Indeed, there is some

tension in her relationship with her mother, and it has crystallised around issues of time, presence/absence and physical self-representation.

Kamlabehn dressed in a manner which was remarkable given her sex, her age and the Hindu nationalist context. She wore trousers (usually blue jeans), an oversized man's shirt or a khadi kurta, and sneakers or men's kolhapuris. These items were selectively drawn from male attire including from within two representational systems exterior to the one considered proper by family and friends for Hindu nationalist women: one was western (trousers, shirts, sneakers) and the other Gandhian (khadi kurta). But, I shall argue, in Kamlabehn's conception of things they had little to do with their original semiotic. Her particular use of what appeared as imitation was such that the "imitated", once displaced into her representational system, was reproduced there as an original. The western items no longer signified the West, the Gandhian items were no longer connected to Gandhianism. This first became clear to me as I observed Kamlabehn's clothes being noticed and commented upon by others in her context. Men, and in particular her father, were indifferent to her dress. Her critics were mainly elderly women family members (her mother and aunts), the people directly in charge of socialising her, including controlling her representation of her sexuality, and who represented themselves as models for her to emulate. They were "bothered" by her dress not so much because of its origin in extra-Hindu representational systems, but rather primarily because they presumed she was violating what they had constructed as the "naturalness" of the sari (or kurta pajama) for Hindu women. Indeed, the critics were right. She was attempting to create for herself a new structural position to occupy: that of a resolutely single, but tough and respected woman who would impose herself in the public space without definite sexual, gender or (Indian) regional connotations. When once her mother complained about her clothes in front of both of us, Kamlabehn turned to me to say, "What nonsense. So many of our goddesses are half-naked. You tell me, what difference does dress make to a real Hindu woman?"

During the period of her engineering studies, Kamlabehn devoted much time to the Samiti, and spent a great deal of it in the company of an elderly Samiti leader, Nilabehn. The two women developed a very close relationship. With her father's express approval and her mother's tolerance, Kamlabehn often spent weekends with the elderly sevika to do Samiti work. The precondition for this freedom was that she keep good grades. Over time, she extended the time devoted to the Samiti and began spending weeknights at Nilabehn's.

In one of her classes at engineering school, Kamlabehn encountered a young man whom she would most often refer to as "a dedicated swayamsevak", and began to meet him off and on. They sometimes studied together, and sometimes "met to discuss politics". After they had known each other for approximately one year, he proposed to her. She was "surprised", and immediately refused: "I told him, I am already married to the Samiti. I am married to the Nation, not to any man." She went on to explain that she had decided to become a pracharika (single, celibate full-time volunteer for the Samiti). He respectfully accepted to continue to think of her as a sister, and according to her, held her in even greater regard.

In the Sangh-Samiti perceptual grid, the position of pracharika is a prestigious one; it implies a high level of skills, a strong personality, the capacity to take on responsibility and to live humbly. Pracharikas are responsible for moving into new areas, establishing new shakhas, training other sevikas in physical and/or intellectual skills, organising campaigns and carrying them through. They must be able to defend themselves physically, for they are expected to travel, often alone, on public transport (trains, buses, etc.). The pracharikas I have met have all impressed me as particularly assertive and serious. Not one ever expressed regret at "giving up" a householder's life. Kamlabehn, at that point, seemed a perfect candidate for such a position.

Beyond Kamlabehn, the existence of pracharikas raises a number of questions about the Samiti's capacity to include a range of personality types and lifestyles. The post has several indirect functions: one is to provide a legitimate space for revolt against the Reproduction-of-the-Same (lifestyle of their mothers, grandmothers, and so on in their feminine genealogies). Here, the woman who chooses independence through celibacy, dedication to other women (the Samiti) and an ideal (the Hindu Nation) in place of dedication to an individual male, her own spatial mobility and the process of becoming a space-for-herself over functioning as a space for a man to come home to,[21] is valorised and provided with the means to realise such choices, albeit solely within the parameters carved out by the organisation.

Kamlabehn and the "dedicated swayamsevak" graduated from engineering school with high marks. He found a job with an engineering company in Bombay but Kamlabehn was unable to find one anywhere because "people prefer men engineers". Eventually, she obtained part-time employment as a science teacher at a local school. She expressed contentment at being able to earn but complained that she did not earn much. The wages were sufficient to support her while she lived partially at her natal home and partly with Nilabehn. The hours were not demanding. As a result she had extended stretches of time to travel around the country "to give service to the Samiti and our Nation".

Religion

Kamlabehn's journeys across India occupy a place in her life akin to pilgrimage for the deeply spiritual. However, since she is not inclined towards spirituality she, in accordance with her own semiotic, invests them with a non-spiritual, political meaning. They are important time/spaces of her "self-realisation" as a Hindu nationalist woman. In them she enacts her right to spatial mobility, thereby directly challenging the de facto rule that traditional upper caste middle class women should be confined to the domestic space or protected by male family members in the public space. The travels also function as a mode of establishing her status in the organisation and her distinction from her natal environment. They sometimes reflect an unconscious aggressive stance against her parents for not socialising her enough in "Hindu culture".

One trip in particular made a lasting impression on Kamlabehn and it was exceptionally revelatory of her relation to Hinduism: in 1985 she went to Manipur "to give a talk" for the Samiti and "discovered Hindu culture. Manipur is the only area I've known that's not polluted by other religions. I grew up in a cosmopolitan city. We don't have our own culture. We are ignorant of Hindu culture." Given her upbringing in an RSS family which is supposedly well-embedded in proper "Hindu culture", the statement can be read as a critique of her natal home and the Sangh-Samiti version of Hindu culture. But, there are several other meanings inherent in it as well. Her comments reflect the essentialist notion that rural spaces constitute the "real India" while urban spaces are aberrations of it. This limited view coincides with colonialist conceptions of rural India as static and staticity as the essence of India. The concept that mixture with other religions is polluting (or otherwise destructive) reflects the binary mode in which the Sangh and the Samiti construct their notions of selfhood, which I shall explain in detail below.

What Kamlabehn stressed about her experience of Manipur was that much of what she had been told about Hinduism earlier was unsubstantiated: "The people eat fish. They're not vegetarians. They don't sit cross-legged like us. They fold their legs into a stooping position to eat. That is Hindu culture. Over here we don't know anything about Hindu culture." Again, her critique of the space she inhabits in Ahmedabad is evident. For Kamlabehn, like a sizeable percentage of Samiti (and Sangh) informants I have interviewed, the ideal is perpetually elsewhere in relation to where they are located. It belongs to another space, or another time, or both, but always to another world in which they are already perpetually displaced as outsiders. The sense of rootlessness combined with an obsessive search for roots is particularly acute among the most active of the sevikas and swayamsevaks I have interviewed, independent of their gender and class.

In Kamlabehn's discourse, "Hindu culture" and "Hindu religion" are nearly synonymous terms. The difference between them is that the former signifies an overall way of life while the latter refers more specifically to a system of representation and a particular class of rituals within that way of life. For Kamlabehn, Hindu religion is "scientific and rational. One can be a Hindu and not believe in any god because Hinduism is a culture and a science of living. Hinduism is scientifically advanced. We had airplanes and helicopters in the time of the Mahabharata and Ramayana." Again, despite the symbolic references Kamlabehn, like some (but certainly not all) sevikas and swayamsevaks, considers belief in gods or goddesses and related rituals as "superstition". Indeed, she informed me that in her family, only her mother "believes in all that and does puja every day".

Kamlabehn's comments should not be taken to mean that she rejects gods and goddesses. On the contrary, she does integrate selected deities in her life: Bharatmata and Ashta Bhuja, as stated above, but also Kali as represented in the *Devi Mahatmya,* or rather as represented in Kamlabehn's interpretation of discussions of the text among sevikas at the upper echelons of the local Samiti hierarchy. Kamlabehn has never read the text herself; in order to understand her mode of relating to the goddesses, one must separate the question of faith from the social and individual functions of the deities as symbolic references.

Bharatmata and Ashta Bhuja have an obvious social role for the organisation and for Kamlabehn within it: they are simply common symbols which bind the sevikas together, and Kamlabehn with them. Beyond that, Bharatmata, Ashta Bhuja and Kali function at the individual level in Kamlabehn's life: they serve as frameworks, as models and as limits, or as Luce Irigaray would probably describe it, as spaces and horizons for the construction of her own ideal identity.[22] Kamlabehn conceptualises each of them diversely and assigns them different roles: Bharatmata provides a (maternal) space for her self-realisation while Ashta Bhuja and Kali provide identity models to emulate. She associates Ashta Bhuja with warrior qualities, and Kali specifically with her role in destroying / neutralising the rakshasas.

Resistance

In Kamlabehn's discourse, the fierce goddesses and other fragments selected from religious discourse are instrumental: one of their functions is to legitimise her unconventional choices while disguising them as points of resistance to normative domesticated femininity. For example, she has managed to render her extreme engagement with the para-military aspects of the Samiti acceptable to initially reluctant family members by formulating them in the language of religion and in conformity with the goals of Hindu nationalism. While all family members encouraged her to learn self-defence, they were not enthusiastic about her intensive involvement with weapons until she "explained things properly". She told them that as a dedicated sevika she needed to travel to do Samiti work, and in order to travel she needed to know self-defence. They fully agreed. Then, she explained that "a woman cannot fight a man with her bare hands alone. And why should I? Did Kali fight the rakshasas with her hands? All our goddesses are armed. Why should I not be armed?"

It is likely that such arguments resonated particularly with the male members of the family, who are accustomed to hearing a similar well-known Sangh slogan: "All our gods are armed." Indeed, its appropriation and feminisation is revelatory of the place of the particular feminine symbolic references in question in the overall Hindu nationalist project. Here the armed goddesses function not as independent femininity but rather as discursive representations of the "other of the Same". That is, they are like the gods and simultaneously the counterparts to the gods, but have no existence independent of them. The inversion (feminine version) of the slogan implies remaining within the context of the male monosexual economy where the ideal qualities and the ultimate goals are those proposed by the Sangh. However, what is important to note for now is Kamlabehn's successful strategic use of the elements in that context to widen her own relative space of freedom within it.

Kamlabehn's mother prefered not to discuss her daughter's paramilitary skills with me, while her father openly expressed pride in his daughter's warrior traits. He seemed almost relieved about them, perhaps because they alleviated some of the fatherly burden of protection. He was fond of stating that she could "take care of herself". One day, during a conversation on violence, like a concerned uncle he asked me if I had ever been "bothered" by men in Delhi. I proceeded to explain that I once was harassed at a bus stop and how I responded, but he cut me short to ask whether or not I had killed the offender. I answered that I did not think it was appropriate to take a life in that situation. With apparent astonishment he began to question me on my capacity to use various arms (knife, gun, rifle). When I told him that I am not in the habit of carrying arms around Delhi, he stated: "Kamla will teach you to shoot if only you can give a few hours a week. You should never be unarmed."

Ultimately, Kamlabehn's paramilitary skills justify her spatial mobility and her spatial mobility justifies her need for the skills. She travels alone second class on trains, in or out of the ladies compartment, and her family "never worries". She maintains that "if any man bothers" her, she will not hesitate to "bash him up". She has had occasion to use her skills "many times. People feel shocked when they see this, a woman who bashes up a man." She has "never killed any, not yet" but has "no fear of killing in self defence", she is "physically and mentally prepared". She feels that if more women would learn self-defence and travel alone, it would become more acceptable and they would be less vulnerable to harassment. Unfortunately, "people think a woman alone on a train is a prostitute. Earlier women from our background could not travel alone, but I am doing this for our Nation. This is how Rashtra Sevika Samiti will change our country." In that sense the Samiti serves as a space where members can escape constraints which otherwise may have been imposed upon them as women within their context. They do so not only without directly rebelling against their environment, but also with its express approval as long as their demands are formulated not in terms of themselves, but rather, in terms of self-sacrifice in the service of a higher common cause, the Hindu Nation.

A second example of Kamlabehn's skill at disguising resistance to norms is in the reversal of her decision concerning marriage. After she and her "dedicated swayamsevak" friend graduated from engineering school and he moved to Bombay, he wrote to her declaring that, like her, "he too would remain celibate". This was not for the Sangh, he explained, but rather because of his fidelity to her, the only woman he had ever been able to envisage as his wife. Kamlabehn "thought about this for a long time". She did not meet him again but they remained in contact periodically by letter. At some point during her travels on Samiti work she fell seriously ill and, for the first time, had nothing to do with herself except think. She realised she could not be happy as a pracharika because she had "emotional needs".

Some time after she recovered, she asked the swayamsevak to visit her in Ahmedabad. Then, in a skilful reversal of the norms in her context (where males dominate and arranged marriage is the rule), she "decided to propose to him, and he accepted". She told her parents only later. They "approved" of her husband, of her decision to marry him and her active role

in carrying it out. Her father rationalised it as his daughter's expression of the wisdom held by those who realise themselves in the Sangh-Samiti set-up: "She has reached the stage where she knows what is best for herself and our Nation. You see that she has chosen a devoted swayamsevak". Indeed, he closely echoed Kamlabehn's own words in describing his new son-in-law. He did not mention it, but the swayamsevak belongs to a similar caste background, and a similar but wealthier class background than Kamlabehn's. Nilabehn integrated the event into her own value system by continuing to nominate it as an "arranged marriage" which, she told me, was "arranged by Kamlabehn...Kamlabehn arranged her own marriage". Having already carved out a space for herself in her environment as a positive embodiment of feminine Hindu nationalist agency, her initiatives, which otherwise might be interpreted as acts of rebellion, were instead perceived as consistent with the ideals in her environment, albeit at times differently by each person concerned.

The effects of marriage on Kamlabehn seemed extreme, but they were mostly external. Her appearance changed abruptly as she abandoned her former attire for a sari, bangles, anklets, bindi. The first time I met her after this change, she explained to me that "this is only for convenience". Indeed, it meant little in terms of her inner landscape or her behaviour in the world. She formulated it thus: "This doesn't matter. Was I any less a woman before this? This dress has not made me a woman. It is a matter of convenience. This is our culture, that women wear this dress." Thus, there was a radical disjunction between the sign of bound feminine energy through her attire (bangles, anklets, etc.) and her discourse on its irrelevance combined with the overwhelming reality of continuity in her pre-to post-marriage conduct. The attire did not change her relationship to spatial mobility or her self-appropriation of her own time. It simply reassured those in her environment by signalling that she occupies a space which in reality she does not. Her new representation of herself can be seen not as a step towards conformity, but rather as part of a strategy in her further legitimation of future potential resistance to norms which matter more to her. It is strategic insofar as it is an easy concession to make. For Kamlabehn, other characteristics, especially behavioural, are not subject to negotiation.

Today, Kamlabehn works as a full-time science teacher in a reputed school outside Ahmedabad while her husband has retained his job in Bombay. She lives in a flat provided by the school, independent of her husband and her family. She meets her husband regularly, but feels "no need to stay together now". He has not become the focal point of her spatial mobility, nor have the roles been reversed. They alternate between meeting in her space and his, and neither "interferes" in the other's activities whether professional or Hindu nationalist. Kamlabehn states that they "will have children if we decide it" but as yet they have not done so. Since marriage, her involvement in the Samiti continues to be a primary factor in her life; she still teaches paramilitary skills and her symbolic references have remained the same. Thus, paradoxically, marriage has been a factor in the expansion of her space of relative freedom. Her family presumes that she no longer needs their collective protection or surveillance for they expect her to come under the individual surveillance of her husband. But in reality, her husband is rarely there and she is not answerable to him. Thus, she is even less directly accountable to others now than earlier.

Revenge

Ultimately, however, Kamlabehn's space of relative freedom has a double meaning and a double function. She pays for it by her entrapment within the walls of Hindu nationalist discourse where she is obliged to be complicit with the Rule of the Hindu male collectivity. The existence of such a space depends directly upon a particular construction of Hindu femininity in relation to "the muslims": the former is fabricated as essentially vulnerable to attacks by the latter. Kamlabehn's self-appropriation of her space/time, her acquisition of skills with weaponry are only justifiable in the name of self-defence (of her own chaste Hindu femininity) and self-sacrifice (for the Hindu Nation where ultimately men rule) against the projected threat constituted by "the muslims".

Such an entity as "the muslims", I shall argue (after Girard and Irigaray),[23] is a required production of the Regime of the Same, of the regime of Hindu nationalist "brothers" who strive to be identical to each other as perfect realised Hindu males. In this scheme, the violence internal to the regime (the self-hatred, the misogyny, the aggressivity and violence which would otherwise run afoul between Hindu males, and between them and Hindu women) is projected onto "the muslims". Indeed, elsewhere I have shown that in the Sangh's publications, it describes the unity of the Hindu Nation as based upon "the knowledge of a common impending enemy".[24] I have also demonstrated that the Sangh's identity models for Muslim males contain characteristics constructed in oppositional terms to those assigned to the model for ideal Hindu males.[25] In that sense, the Sangh displaces the undesirable from within the "Hindu Community" onto

Karen Haydock

a rejectable entity, "the muslims". Finally, it shifts the characteristics it assigns to "the muslims" onto the Muslims and, according to this logic, the violence ascribed to them can only be expelled when the latter are neutralised. In other words, in the Hindu nationalist framework, the acting out of violence against Muslims is a means for the restoration of the internal Hindu nationalist Order.

In Kamlabehn's discourse on Muslims, the Sangh and Samiti discourses are a point of departure. Although they differ on some of the finer details, the two organisations share the notion that Muslim identity is essentially embodied in the Muslim male, while Muslim women are potential objects of communal and (hetero-) sexual appropriation.[26] Further, they both associate "muslimness" fundamentally with the "memory" of violence against Hindus, and the notion of "justice" which is used to legitimise revenge. The "memory" in question however, is selective; it requires forgetting whatever may question the unity or legitimacy of the "Hindu Community". At times the Sangh and Samiti name the original violence as "Muslim invasions"; in other instances it is the "vivisection' of the territory and the rape of Hindu women during Partition. Whatever the case, the "original" violence is always essentialised, and out of it is extracted the notion of "Muslimness". Each subsequent conflict where Hindus and Muslims clash

is constructed in a chain of substitution as metaphorically related to the so-called original violence. In Kamlabehn's discourse, these aspects are personalised through the "memory" of two massive local riots which occurred within the time/space of her life but which she did not personally witness. I would like briefly to explicate these instances, to discuss Kamlabehn's discourse on them, and finally, to arrive at an analysis of their relation to Kamlabehn's space of relative freedom/space of entrapment and their negotiation via her symbolic references.

The first instance took place in Ahmedabad when Kamlabehn was still a child. She refers to it simply as the "1969 Muslim riot" after the year of its occurrence and the entity she deems responsible. In it, 1,500 lives were lost and over 30,000 people (mostly Muslim) were left homeless. Those who suffered, whether Muslims or Hindus, were the most economically destitute of the city's population located in its most crowded quarters, far from Kamlabehn's middle class neighbourhood.

In Ahmedabad, poor women have consistently participated in varying degrees in communal violence (by discreetly gathering stones in shopping bags and the folds of saris during temporary relaxation of curfew, by helping to fabricate gasoline bombs at home and in some instances by throwing them). At that time, however, middle class women did not participate in the actual battles themselves. In contrast, some of the latter were active in post-riot relief work, but Kamlabehn was too young for such activities. In her immediate family, only her elder brother participated in a Sangh relief team designed to aid Hindus affected by the riots.

The second set of riots occurred in 1985-6. The conflict had started in 1985 as caste-based, around the issue of reservation, but by 1986 local Hindu nationalist groups managed to shift its focus to Hindu-Muslim communalism. The riots touched the same population and were concentrated mainly in the same areas of the city as in 1969, except that here they involved a wider range of people. The most significant change in 1985-6 was that, for the first time, Hindu nationalist women of all classes, including middle class members of the Samiti and the related Hindu Mahila Sabha, actively participated in the violence in significant numbers, in a meticulously organised way.[27] Kamlabehn was old enough to participate, but she was absent from Ahmedabad (on Samiti work) when the riots first erupted, and remained so for the duration of the open conflict. In contrast, in between curfews, her brother and father had helped in the Sangh's relief work.

In Kamlabehn's discourse the two sets of riots, albeit separated by a period of sixteen or seventeen years,

are almost indistinguishable. Her "memory" of both sets is mediated by her brother and father's experience, discussions in bauddhik sessions in the Samiti shakha, the opinions of other family members and friends, the Sangh Parivar media coverage, the non-Sangh-Parivar media coverage and the distortionary effects of the passage of time. Her speech and its contents range from calm to agitated in nature, and this is often simply a function of the exigencies of the moment or of the subject matter which leads to the discussion of the riots. Despite this variance, which I shall discuss below, there are a number of constants. For example, she holds onto Hindu nationalist cliches throughout as markers "muslims on the warpath" and "muslim barbarism" are commonly repeated phrases. She also consistently attempts to explain the riots in archetypal terms: "They humiliated our men. They raped our women. They destroyed our property. It was just like Partition all over again."

In her least extreme speech on the riots, which is most often connected to the first set of riots, she says she feels thus about Muslims: "I have nothing against them. Earlier they were Hindus but they turned traitors. They could become Hindus again, but you see what they have done to our people. That is why we don't like them". Here as elsewhere, she differentiates almost unconsciously between her personal attitude as an individual ("I have nothing against them") and her attitude as part of a larger collectivity ("we don't like them"). Indeed, the hatred seems to come into existence when raised to the collective level.

Kamlabehn's most extremely agitated speech is generally reserved for the second set of riots. It is as though the second experience of absence/presence functioned to reinforce and extend the first. She communicates a certain frustration at being (again) in an inappropriate space/time while the battle raged without her. In addition she articulates self-guilt. She expresses it in terms of her positionality in a network of relations within the Hindu People, and her failure to protect the weakest of the latter despite her cultivation of warrior skills.[28] Thus, she asserts that those who suffered most among the Hindus "were the poorest of our people. They were the most backward. They lost everything. They even lost their lives. We did nothing to save them from the Muslims. I was outside." Her guilt is clearly based on notions of her personal failure to fulfil her duty, and not on a self-critique of her caste-class position. Indeed, here as elsewhere, she rationalises the latter by adhering to the Sangh-Samiti presupposition of the inherent "backwardness" of the poor, the counterpart of which is the notion of her own "merit". Further, in this instance the "we" of the Hindu community which "did nothing" is placed in a relationship of disjointed identity to the "I"

who could do nothing because she was absent from Ahmedabad.

In her most intensely aggressive renderings. Kamlabehn makes use of the same cliches, some of which I have cited above, and connects them in an associational chain which progresses from notions of Muslim violence to Hindu humiliation to threats of revenge. In our dialogues, often it was the very mention of Muslims as possible victims that provoked her rage. For example, when I specifically asked her about the fate of Muslims in the 1986 riots she replied with anger: "Why do you ask about them? Look at what they have done to our people. They deserve to die. They should all be killed. They spill our blood. They rape our women. Let their blood be spilled, the bloody bastards. Just as Kali did not spare even one rakshas." The statements are polysemic, and this is not the place to provide an exhaustive reading of them. However, for now we can note that they reveal Kamlabehn's construction of Muslims as sexually aggressive to women, as the illegitimate offspring of Bharatmata, as the origin of violence, and therefore deserving of destruction through bleeding. The preoccupation with blood and bodily dismemberment suggests the paranoiac mechanisms at work in Hindu nationalist discourse in general.

Indeed, in Kamlabehn's mind, to kill a Muslim is to fulfil one's archetypal duty as a militant Hindu

दीन धर्म का पहला पाठ
मैंने ही तो सिखलाया था
धर्म के नाम पर औरत की
इज्जत लूटना कब सिखलाया था।

woman. She constructs it as a divine act modelled upon and explicable via Kali's ridding the world of evil in the form of demons in the *Devi Mahatmya*. She rationalises anti-Muslim violence by Hindu women as a just act of direct revenge provoked by Muslim male sexual violation of Hindu femininity and womanhood. However, when questioned about her personal experiences with Muslim males, Kamlabehn states that she has never met any. Further, in her daily life, the only sexual harassment she has been subject to has been by Hindu males. She explains that "among Hindus there are some who are not yet conscious. That is why we need RSS, to teach them to respect women." Further, in a rare critique of the Sangh, Kamlabehn admits that even in the Sangh "there are some who do not respect women". There is never, however, the same emotional charge, the same anger when speaking of Hindu men; In that sense, she has more or less split masculinity into two; the Hindu male who is essentially decent (unconscious Hindu males exist but are rare and always less threatening than any Muslim male), and Muslim males who are essentially aggressive and violent, including sexually. These constructions are of an arbitrary nature; their very existence depends solely upon the Hindu nationalist context and what therein is designated as an acceptable object of hatred for Hindu nationalist women. Indeed, by projecting such characteristics onto Muslim men, Kamlabehn is able to discharge emotion that might otherwise accumulate into (an impossible, unacceptable) rebellion against the macho Hindu men in her environment. Such an attitude functions to confine Hindu nationalist women within a "Hindu Community" whose boundaries and landscape are defined essentially by Hindu nationalist men.

Some concluding remarks

In Kamlabehn's discourse, obviously, the role of the divine is not to be divine at all, but rather, to enable her to work our two inter-related aspects of her identity within the Hindu nationalist context: fierce femininity and her anti-macho stance. The former, as I have demonstrated, is articulated in terms of the warrior goddess, Kali, in the Devi Mahatmya, the latter in terms of the demons Kali neutralises in the same text. The anti-macho stance can only be partial; the enemy is displaced from communally-unmarked masculine violence and aggressivity onto the person of Muslim men.

Kamlabehn's discourse, her use of the symbolic to further a non-spiritual agenda and the resistance/revenge motifs are not particular to Hindu nationalism. They are part of a larger contemporary tendency in which religion has come to be instrumentalised to deliver meaning in an increasingly meaningless environment. Thus, for example, some urban middle class perceptions of dislocated identities are reflected in the multiplication of new "modern" and as yet non-politicised sects. Similarly, representations of women's ideal identity are steadily shifting to include forceful qualities and resistance / revenge motifs. The latter are produced, for example, again at the symbolic level, in a new genre of film in which women are portrayed as avenging villains to defend family and community "honour".[29] Indeed, none of this necessarily signifies liberation for women. The feminine agency in question, independently of the symbolic references which are made to intervene to justify it, is modelled upon machismo and exists for men (to defend male-dominated family or community "honour" or their Hindu nationalist project). Thus, in the final analysis, the space of relative freedom, the refuge from masculine domination provided by certain symbolic elements, collapses under the reality of the male-dominated framework which surrounds it. In the meantime, it functions as a buffer-zone in which women such as Kamlabehn work out aspects of their spatial / temporal mobility while simultaneously adhering to their own ultimate negation.

Notes

[1] I would like to thank Tanushree Gangopadhyay, Gita Shah, Rita Malik and Sangeeta Shroff of Chingari Nari Sangh, Ahmedabad, for their contributions to my interview process in the earliest phase, in 1986. I am grateful to Veena Das for meaningful discussions and encouragement from 1988 onwards. I am also grateful to Sanjeeb Dattachaudhary and Rajendra Pradhan for their sensitive feedback during and following my fieldwork. My thanks to Amrita Basu for her thorough reading and helpful suggestions, and finally, my deep debt to Maureen L.P. Patterson for her insightful commentary.

[2] See, for example, Andrea Dworkin, *Right Wing Women* (New York: Coward-McCann Inc., 1978).

[3] Kathleen M. Blee, *Women of the Klan: Racism and Gender in the 1920s* (Berkeley: University of California Press, 1991).

[4] Claudia Koonz, *Mothers in the Fatherland: Women, the Family and Nazi Politics* (New York: St. Martin's Press, 1987).

[5] The names of the informant and those in her entourage have been changed to protect the privacy of all concerned, and because I do not wish to be at the origin of a witch-hunt which would target one or two individuals while missing the point as to why women adhere to Hindu nationalism.

[6] The interviews were non-directive, conversational, sporadic in time. The first two took place in a collective atmosphere where another sevika and an Ahmedabadi friend of mine were present. Later, I conducted them alone.

[7] Paola Bacchetta, "On the Construction of Identities in a Hindu Nationalist Discourse: The Rashtriya Swayamsevak Sangh and the Rashtra Sevika Samiti", (original in French), forthcoming Ph.D dissertation, Université de Paris I, France.

[8] I use the term "the muslims" in the lower case, in quotes and in the plural to designate a non-entity, a projection, in the sense of Hitler's "the jews", as understood by Jean-Francois Lyotard in his *Heidegger and "the jews* (Minneapolis: University of Minnesota Press, 1990). Lyotard

argues that the term "the jews" stands in for the unrepresentable in western thought, for what is Forgotten in it, for the debt the West does not acknowledge and cannot repay and so must destroy. The term "the muslims" in the Sangh and Samiti discourse similarly stands in for what is unrepresentable in the "Hindu community", but also for what the Sangh believes must be sacrificed by it in order to conserve the integrity of the "community" itself. Thus the term does not signify real Muslims; rather, it stands in for them and displaces them. In the Samiti's, the Sangh's and Kamlabehn's discourse it functions as a screen upon which the fantasy of evil threatening the integrity of the Hindu Nation is projected.

9 The Sangh has been the object of much research by social scientists, and several monographs on the organisation exist. For a critical overview of them, an alternative historiography of the Sangh and a first historiography of the Samiti, see my dissertation, cited above.

10 Interview with Samiti officer Promila Mehta carried out by the author in March 1990, at the Samiti headquarters in Nagpur, Maharashtra.

11 For an analysis of the processes, sources and logic at work in the construction of the Sangh and Samiti's discourses, as well as of divergence where gender is concerned, see Paola Bacchetta, "Different Choices/Different Voices: the Rashtriya Swayamsevak Sangh, the Rashtra Sevika Samiti and Their Respective Concepts of the Hindu Nation", forthcoming in Kumari Jayawardena (ed.), *Women, the State and Cultural Identity* (New Delhi: Kali for Women).

12 Ibid.

13 The creation of Ashta Bhuja and her symbolism is discussed in a number of Samiti publications. See especially Rashtra Sevika Samiti, *Karmayogini vom Mausiji, Rashtra Sevika Samiti ki Sansthapika Pramukh Sanchalika, Srimati Lakshmibai Kelkar ki Jivani* (Nagpur: Sevika Prakashan 1989).

14 Preface to Rashtra Sevika Samiti- Organisation of Hindu Women (Nagpur: Sevika Prakashan, undated but post 1978).

15, 16, 17, Ibid.

18 The text of the prayer is printed in a variety of publications. See, for example, *Deep Stambh, Rashtra Sevika Samiti Akhil Bharatiya Trayopdesh Traivarshik Sammelan,*1986 (Nagpur: Sevika Prakashan, 1986).

19 This is based on interviews I carried out with sevikas from 1986 to 1990 in Ahmedabad, Nagpur and Pune.

20 Gananath Obeysekere, *Medusa's Hair: An Enquiry on Personal Symbols and Religious Experience* (Chicago: University of Chicago Press, 1981),pp. 22, 27.

21 Luce Irigaray, *Ethique de la difference sexuelle,* (Paris: Ed. de Minuit, 1984). Irigaray argues that women in contexts of male domination have no space of their own. As mothers, women represent a space for men's self-realisation; as wives they subsist in movement towards the Other (the husband). A precondition for gender equality is woman's appropriation of herself and of a space/time-for-her-self. The position of pracharak allows women a certain form of detachment from the individual male (as husband)and modifies their relationship to space within the overall male-dominated Hindu nationalist context.

22 See Irigaray, *Sexes et Parentes* (Paris: Les Editions de Minuit, 1987).

23 Irigaray's reading of Rene Girard's text on sacrifice has served as a point of departure for my reflections here. See Irigaray, *Sexes et Parentes,* op.cit.; Rene Girard, *La violence et le sacre* (Paris: Bernard Grasset, 1972).

24, 25 See my dissertation, cited above.

26 For an analysis of the Sangh's conception of Muslim women, see Paola Bacchetta, "Communal Property/Sexual Property: On Representations of Muslim Women in a Hindu Nationalist Discourse", in Zoya Hasan (ed.), *Forging Identities: Gender, Communities and the State* (New Delhi: Kali for Women, 1994).

27 Hindu nationalist women's agency in the 1985-6 riots has been documented and analysed in Paola Bacchetta, "From

the Mother Goddess to the Warrior: On the Shifting Place of Women in Communal Riots and Communalist Discourse in Contemporary Ahmedabad, Gujarat", (original in French; M. Phil. Thesis in Sociology, Paris, France, 1986). Also, on middle class women actors against reservations in the 1985 riots, see Ila Joshi, "Women and Anti-Reservation Stir in Ahmedabad", and Chingari Nari Sangh, "Impact of Caste and Communal Riots of Ahmedabad on Women" (paper presented at the National Conference of Women's Studies,Chandigarh, 1986).

28 In an insightful article on the 1984 Delhi-area riots against the Sikhs after the assassination of Indira Gandhi, Veena Das discusses the emotional states, including guilt, of Sikh women survivors. Das explains that the survivors articulate this guilt in terms of their perceived failure to protect their men and to properly accomplish the last religious rites after death in cases where the bodies were not recoverable. In that sense, the guilt is structured relationally, in terms of the survivors' perceived duty as wives. Kamlabehn's guilt, albeit in absentia, is similarly constructed around her perception of her failure to accomplish her self-designated duty of protection, but also around her consciousness of her own material privileges in relation to the dead. In Kamlabehn's case the relation is to the anonymous members of the "Hindu People" for whom she feels it is her duty to sacrifice herself (and her material belongings). See Veena Das, "Our Work to Cry, Your Work to Listen" in Das (ed.), *Mirrors of Violence: Communities, Riots and Survivors in South Asia* (Delhi: Oxford University Press, 1990).

29 Some of these include *Sherni, Zakhmi Aurat, Mera Shikar, Gunahon ka Phaisla, Aag ke Sholay.* For a discussion of films in which women are represented in terms of revenge, see M. Rahman, "Hindi Films, Women Strike Back",*India Today*, July 5, 1988; Madhu Kishwar & Ruth Vanita, "Male Fantasies of Female Revenge", *Manushi*, September/October 1988.

Fighting on all fronts

an interview with K., a peasant leader of Sindhiani Tehrik, Sindh

You go from village to village in the course of your work. What do you talk about to the women you meet?

We talk about the injustice and oppression that Sindhi women have faced for centuries, the exploitation and the physical violence. Women have come to accept this as normal — we say they should not. They should unite, they should sit together and talk about their problems and then try and find some solutions. To win their confidence we make friends with them. We help if a child has a problem in school, or if someone needs to be admitted to hospital, for example. Only after some time and effort are the women ready to sit with us.

Do those who perpetrate the injustices on women use Islam to justify them?

Yes. When they wish to control a woman they say she must observe purdah, she is not allowed this and not permitted the other. Once I went to a certain village where the *wadera* (feudal lord), a big man, wanted us to hold our meeting in his house, not because he sympathised with our cause, but because he thought he would gain more respect for it. We did not want to go there but his wife sent word that she was very ill and we should come to the house for her sake.

She told us that though the *wadera* could afford it he did not send her to Karachi or Hyderabad where she could be properly treated. He sent for a woman from the nearby village, Who was little more than a nurse, because he said Islam did not allow women to be attended by male doctors. But the wadera himself met all the women he wanted and also engaged in immoral acts.

We were upset to hear that he used Islam both to justify his own immoral conduct and to deny his wife proper medical attention. In such circumstances women start feeling guilty and believe that they are really doing something wrong. Many become resigned to their condition and become silent, some become psychological cases.

We are told to stay in the *chadar aur chardivari* (behind the veil, within the four walls of the house), we are told not to venture out. There is no legal freedom, we have seen that it is non-existent. They use religion to do as they please.

They make children do what they want by using religion. The same is true of the government. What did Zia-ul Haq do? And what is this Shariat Bill? And what do these waderas and jagirdars (landlords) do?

But you must have shared this kind of upbringing - what was the situation in your family?

My paternal grandfather used to pray five times a day. But he was not a pir (religious leader). He never oppressed the villagers, and he never forced the women of his household to pray. he was criticised by the villagers for this, but he said we were free to decide for ourselves, to do it if we felt the need.

My maternal grandfather started a maktab (school) where he used to read Shah Latif's poetry. He did not pray, but emphasised the need to be a good person, whether or not the rituals of religion were performed. He felt that it was useless to put up a facade of being a good Muslim if you were corrupt inside.

Did your grandfather educate his children?

Yes, my mother studied at home. Some girls went out to learn to read and write. My mother did not like us to fast when we were children. We did it for fun sometimes. Relatives used to tell me to pray. When my brother was arrested we were all told to pray. For three months we prayed for him. Then one night we said this would be the last night of prayer, and if it worked our faith would be strong. My aunt scolded me. She said that this was an awful attitude. My mother disagreed. Her sisters would always say that it was our irreligious behaviour that had sent my brother to jail, that had prompted my brothers to learn English, and for me and my sisters to have turned out "bad". "Other girls are very religious, they pray, they stay away from evil!"

Why was your mother different, considering they were brought up together?

My mother had a very tough life, she was an orphan. She never saw her mother. Her father died of TB. One of the elder sisters raised her. She, with some other girls, used to take sheep to graze in the woods. My father fell in love with my mother. My mother said that when my father saw her grazing her sheep her clothes were torn to tie things up in and the girls were singing. He came by on his horse and asked her name. She said her name was Lali, and he said that was Raja Dahir's wife's name too. He then told her to go and ask her father to marry her to him. She was 13. My grandfather was very angry and he refused, because my father already had a wife. The nikah (marriage) had been performed when they were children, as happened often.

What about your father?

My father used to pray like my grandfather. When people asked him why he didn't make his family do the same, he would say that his family could decide for themselves. If they wanted to, they would, if not, it would ultimately be their problem.

What is your faith?

From childhood one sees things and has certain hopes. Children learn from what they hear around them and pick up much from society. Many times they are told not to argue, to just accept. I was treated the same way. I was always told that He cannot be seen, but He does exist. He created the world. There has to be a Creator because nothing appears by itself. The beds we slept on were made by others, plants would grow, things would happen — something was making them happen. Then I read some books. I read that there is matter. That too has come from somewhere, but the last stage never came.

What do you mean by the last stage? Are you a believer?

I am, yet I am not. My mother's and father's and my own beliefs are different. There was a conflict inside. Sometimes I thought things happened by themselves, and other times I felt there had to be a Creator. If there is one, where is He/She/It? The manifestation of this Creator is in the universe. Sometimes I think there is no such Creator. We have just been programmed to fear. People were scared of things: of water, light, witches. Then they suggested there is an Allah whom you must fear.

Do you think of Allah when you think of such things, or just a creator? Do you go via Islam?

No, this has nothing to do with Islam, but it is the battle inside which continues. Things are evolving, changing all around ... Personally, I am very broadminded, progressive, liberal.

How have you brought up your children?

My children are totally free. They are not cowards like me, they take things on, they don't avoid sensitive subjects.

But you do participate in the usual traditions — someone's death, weddings ...

Yes ... and we listen to them preaching fear ... They talk of the terrible fires of hell—telling us to be scared of the day of judgement. It is an awful atmosphere. I feel that the women listening to this may die. But they survive!

Will your daughters find their own husbands?

Yes, definitely, they are completely free. I will not make the decision.

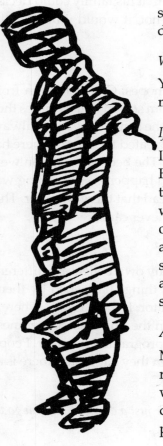

If your husband stood in your way, what would you do?

I would leave him. What would he do: tie me up? He has never done anything like that. If he ever says that it is unfair to him that I am not always there when he returns from work, and complains about our marriage, my children defend me. They think I am doing the right thing. They tell him that he should not talk like that, that I control my own life, and am able to tell right from wrong myself. My sons and daughters both take my side.

Are your colleagues in Sindhiani believers?

Most of the members of Sindhiani Tehrik are very religious. It makes no difference to the organisation whether or not these women pray. As far as I am concerned, I don't think there is any compulsion to pray. Who knows what it is? When we talk about it,

I find their thoughts are the same as everyone else's. Sometimes we disagree and sometimes not, when we sit around discussing it. Some women come and quote from the Koran and claim that people call the Sindhiani women kafirs (unbelievers). So there is a problem. We debate it.

Have there ever been such heated arguments that women have had to leave?

No, not for this reason. But let me tell you about an interesting experience. There was a woman , a maulani (excessively religious) who used to call women over to read the Koran. It was a good place to socialise and gossip. This woman used to address them and tell them how they must bear all pain in silence, how men were their pirs, and so on.

We went to see her, because her influence in the villages was undermining Sindhiani's work. We met some women who had good potential. We worked with them but we couldn't stay there all the time. So we went to this woman and asked her how she saw things. She said she was glad we had come to discuss this with her. She was very nice.We said that women had been in the forefront of all struggle, war, etc. It was not our business to question their religion — that was their personal decision. We said we didn't care if the woman was Hindu, kafir or Muslim, and we asked her to cooperate with us. She told us she'd think about it and get back to us the next day. The next few times we went she agreed to come with us on our visits to different units. I suppose she thought she would preach her version of Islam to these women too. But the women spoke of poverty and she began to change her mind. The girls told her about their problems, cried out their frustrations, and this woman came back and agreed that our society does subject women to a lot of hardships and we never pay attention to them. Our religion tells us to have patience, accept oppression quietly and without complaint. We took this woman on half a dozen trips and even asked her to speak once. The issue was the marriage of a young girl who had been forced to marry against her will. They had beaten her so much that she was badly hurt. This woman spoke incredibly well and even started crying. We were very surprised. Then we realised she would work with us. Due to her influence a few villages where our work had been stopped, began working again. She is now one of us. She still prays, but does not preach or go overboard.

There are lots of things in the Koran and Sunnah that do not apply to men and women equally. But maulvis (self-appointed priests), society and the State preach this inequality and call Sindhiani women kafirs since Sindhiani demands equal rights. Doesn't this cause problems for the members since they are believers?

The question does arise in our committee, but if the Koran preaches equal rights, that is just words. They have realised that these are just words to throw at us, and are not interpreted and acted upon as we would like. The Koran has been interpreted by men from their own perspective, not ours. We speak about this in our Central Committee.

We should read translations by women, and even get a woman who knows Arabic to translate accurately for us. Religion is very influential in rural areas. Oppression is justified through religion, and the women have been made to accept it. Obviously, they want to discuss this so they can do something. They feel helpless and bound — they want to move forward, improve things.

But Sindhiani hasn't addressed religion in its mobilisation. Inspite of this, you have some 50,000 members. So why do you need to make an issue of religion now?

Well, our members are religious . . . We have not addressed religion because our issues are different. However, when the mullahs and *waderas* in Sanghar lock up their women in the name of religion, obviously women resent this and would like to be able to present a different argument. Then this does become an issue. Various mullahs have announced from mosques that the Sindhiani Tehrik women are this and that . . . they are kafirs. Wherever they go they have caused women to come out of their homes and lose their faith. But we have won over our opponents wherever we have gone. Nobody criticises or taunts Sindhiani women now. We are, therefore, not too affected. There was a man in this village we were working in, who wanted to know where we went with young girls and how we conducted ourselves. He was a maulvi, so we asked him to come with us. We told him we had an open programme that day and he was welcome to watch. When the women started talking, he said there was nothing objectionable in what we were doing, the fatwas (edicts passed by priests) were wrong. He said we were doing good work, but we shouldn't travel (in buses, etc.) as much as we did! He even let his own women join us. But it is true that we have never really addressed the issue of religion. We have only touched upon it when it has been necessary, and that too on an individual basis, not as an organisation. If a village is into religion, we use religion to justify what we do, but only on an individual basis. We give references of Muslim women who did great things, like Bibi Ayesha.

But the men who support Sindhiani (like that maulvi) . . . aren't they supporting you because you talk of Sindh, an issue close to their hearts?

No, we talked of women, and when that maulvi came with us he heard women express the desire to be educated, to be granted their rights and not be treated like animals. And maulvis themselves aren't great people, they aren't interested in anyone's problems. On the surface they are angels — long white beards, white clothes and the tasbee (beads). But inside the home, they yell at their wives, they become vicious animals. Their mothers and sisters, wives and daughters see them behaving like angels on the streets with the name of Allah always on their lips, and then watch them oppress them at home. They watch and wonder and invariably become rebellious.

Have the women in the villages ever said that you work against the principles of Islam?

Of course people say we are kafir, but the women have never said it. There were a few, like the one we convinced to work with us . . .

But suppose you go into a new village tomorrow. When you have your first meeting in the village, don't people say you're non-Muslim, and criticise you for being out of your homes?

Yes, they do, and we defend ourselves by giving examples from religion itself. We manage to face them. We tell them that there are so many problems—that their daughters may get caught in the web of all this — we tell them of the troubles of other women. They talk of the need for schools and health facilities. Is that wrong? Is it wrong that we come out of our homes and try to help our sisters? There is a lot of talk about how traditions are a part of religion — these traditions are like knives at our throats, they suffocate us. They mix religion with tradition, saying that our marriages and lives are predetermined, we are helpless . . . They say that is our religion.

It is said that you sometimes prevent marriages from taking place at the last minute. Once

you even brought the bride home because she did not consent to the nikah. Is this so?

Yes, we brought her with us. The baraat was there, people were singing. In the excitement of the moment, we didn't realise it, but now it seems really weird! They asked her, she didn't reply, and everyone began congratulating each other as if the nikah had been performed.

We have heard that Sindhiani have also fought for the rights given to women in Islam and have used these to advance the cause of women. Can you give examples?

One was the marriage of my sister's daughter. My sister is a sensible woman. She belongs to an educated family and is quite progressive, but when it came to her daughter's marriage she became very traditional. When they came to ask the girl if she was willing to accept the son of so and so as her husband, the girl remained quiet, but my sister, who was standing behind, said yes! They asked a second and a third time. The girl did not say a word, but the mother approved the man, and everyone said the girl had given her consent and the nikah had been performed!

I was not there at the time but when I came I was told what had happened. I called the girl and asked her if this was true, and she said yes. I asked her if she wished to marry the man and she said no. What kind of acceptance was this when the girl had not said yes? But the witnesses had accepted the nikah as valid, the girl had become a victim of our traditions.

I called more people and asked them and they said the nikah had been performed and that this K. is a rebel and a trouble-maker. She wants to harm our village. She will damage the future of this girl because no one will want to marry her.

Then I took the girl and went to Maulvi Abdul

Latif of Thatta, whom I know a little. I told him how the marriage had been performed and he said I should bring two people from the bridegroom's family to him. The bridegroom and his mother were not ready to come with us but the elder brother-in-law came. We asked him whether the nikah had been performed and he said yes. The entire panchayat (committee of village elders) had witnessed it and so had the mother and father. Then the groom's mother was asked to swear on the Koran that she had heard it herself and she said no. She had been outside at the time. Then the maulvi asked me to bring my sister, but she was not ready to come with us. We explained to her that if the maulvi ruled that the marriage was valid it would be the end of the matter, if not, then it would be in her interest to do something about it. So she came.

The girl was asked to swear with her hand on the Koran that she had agreed to accept the marriage. Thrice she was asked and thrice she denied having given her consent. When asked who had consented, she said her mother had, on her behalf. At this the maulvi said the nikah was not valid. I asked him to give his ruling in writing but he said he would first place his decision in front of two or three other maulvis to get their approval. Then I went after eight or ten days and got it from him in writing.

What are the kinds of excesses committed against women and how has Sindhiani dealt with them?

There is the matter of the nikah, and there are many other problems. Women are beaten up by husbands, they are threatened with divorce. As a result sometimes the women leave the husbands and seek refuge with their parents. But if their parents won't protect them, or are too poor, then they come to Sindhiani. We discuss each issue at our meetings and, if necessary, also at the Awami Tehrik meetings. Some of us are also members of the Awami Tehrik. When they fail we bring the woman away and keep her in our home for five or six months. Sometimes it may take upto two years before matters are sorted out.

You keep them in your own home?

Yes, they come and work with me in the different units. We talk and listen to ghazals at night. Just two or three months ago there was a woman in my house already when another came. She had been beaten up and also burnt slightly. She was making roti when her husband dragged her by the hair and beat her up. I brought her home. Then a third woman also arrived. Two of them had children. How long could their husbands cook, feed the children and clean the house? One of the husbands sent his children, five or six of them, to me with the message that as I was looking after his wife I may as well keep the children

too, feed them, clothe them and send them to school!

At last the grandfather was embarrassed. He scolded his son and told him to bring his wife home because she would not come back otherwise. He came three times and begged and pleaded. Then I sent his wife with him. Then the husband of the second came when I was not home. He wept and pleaded with his wife to return but she said she could not do so without the consent of the sister who had given her protection. He protested that it was none of my business, but his wife was adamant. Then he came to me and we stipulated certain conditions which he had to fulfil, and we also asked him to bring some other people with him. He brought a few neighbours with him, and then we sent his wife back.

So you reconcile the couple. But what if a reconciliation does not take place? What happens to the woman then?

Usually there is a reconciliation. Only in one case was it not possible, so we helped the woman to obtain a divorce and then to marry again. We say if you like the man, it's your business whether he beats you or whatever. If you don't want to put up with it, then we intervene. If your parents are too poor, fend for yourself however difficult your life may be.

Do the parents take girls back in Sindh? They don't in the Punjab.

Yes, they do, so the women can go home. But if the parents are really poor, then they don't take them back because they're afraid. It is the pretty girls of poor families who marry *waderas* who suffer the most at their hands. Their parents cry for them but don't keep them, so we try and give them the confidence and strength they need. We take responsibility for them.

Then there was this woman who had been divorced, and we supported her. People said we had instigated the entire thing and taken her away from her home. We talked to them, it became an issue in the Awami Tehrik. Now the woman who is divorced feels that it is no disgrace and society will accept her.

Men marry several times in Sindh. What does Sindhiani feel about this?

We have stopped this practice. Let's see how they do it now!

How do you stop them?

We make a lot of noise. We go and talk to the girl's family and try and convince them that this is cruelty. If he already has a wife, he just wants more "labour". There is a man in one of these villages, whenever work in his fields slackens, he advises his sons to get married again. But things are changing. The grandson was going to take his fifth wife — they're young girls—so we went to see them. I asked them if they were happy and if their husbands loved them all. They answered yes. Later I discovered that they work so much they don't know what is happening around them, that they are victims of oppression. They work like animals, and can only think of when they will find a few moments to rest. The concept of happiness and love between husband and wife have no place in such a life.

I sat them down to talk, and their brother-in-law, an engineer, showed up. He said his salaams and asked what lessons I was teaching them! I asked him to sit down as well. Then I asked them in turn whether they thought this was a just situation. The girls wouldn't say a word, so I asked the engineer if he thought having five wives was a decent arrangement. He said well, no, but they are all very happy, leading a good life. I told him that they had no time to think about their lives. Even now they were probably not listening to us, but waiting till we finished so that they could go and rest. He then said that he did not think men should take so many wives, but it was a tradition. I asked if he had ever disagreed with his father and he said his father would not listen. I said, has you mother ever said anything? Have you got a group of men together to talk about it? You are a respected engineer, have you ever objected? So he said his mother couldn't say anything in defiance of his father and he had never raised the subject either. I asked if I could talk to his wife, and he said yes. She said she was happy. I asked the engineer to leave and then his wife opened up and started talking, which encouraged the others to talk as well! Then, when I spoke to the man, he agreed with me. I said just make five men sweep and clean and cook and work in the fields — they would take five days leave afterwards! You are an educated man, you should understand. Then we heard he was getting married again. We went and tried to dissuade him, we also asked the girl not to agree to the marriage and it didn't take place.

What about the Sindhi, or even Pakistani, practice of marrying girls to the Koran?

Waderas, jagirdars and Syeds (descendants of the Prophet) do this to save their property and keep it within the family. In Thatta, there is a Shirazi family where six or seven sisters are old women now, married to the Koran. They dress up, wear jewellery and just stay at home because they have nowhere to go. The weddings are very lavish with all the trappings of usual weddings. If the daughter is *gaddi nasheen* (heir to religious title and property) even the father bows before her.

So daughters can be gaddi nasheen here?

Yes, *waderas* give a lot of gold, all that also goes to the father. At first the girl is impressed by all the attention, but then she becomes disillusioned and ends up a mental case.

What does Sindhiani think of this whole Islamisation issue and of the new laws that have been introduced? The Shariat Bill for example?

We discuss it; Sindhiani members do not like laws of this kind because they feel they will further incapacitate women. They have enough problems as it is. But this Law of Evidence for instance . . . our women are not educated, how can they go to court? Their future is decided by the *wadera* or her husband or brother-in-law. Anyone can decide her fate. What is left for her to decide in court? But if the matter should arise concerning one of our girls or women, then we will take up the issue and make a noise.

Do you not mention Islam in your manifesto at all?

No, we don't, but all of us agree on our manifesto. We have openly stated that we have no religion but humankind. And we do take a stand against the Law of Evidence, qisas, polygamy ...

Are Sindhiani members Muslims only?

No, there are many Hindus.

Isn't this a problem?

Yes, it's a very big issue. About a year and a half ago Hindu women boycotted Sindhiani, on their own, not because their men made them do it, because they wouldn't eat or drink from anyone else's vessels. There were about 50 women in all, Hindus, Maighvar and Bagri women. The Muslims too started doing the same thing. So, next time we told everyone to bring their own glasses. Muslim women also brought their own. There were four separate matkas (pitchers of water) for the Hindus, Maighvar, Bagri and Muslims. A woman from my village, Zainab, got up and said everyone would drink a little from each one. She told me to get up and give everyone a sip of water from each matka. I was a bit hesitant because it was a sensitive issue, but she encouraged us. She said we were all equal, all women with the same problems, all Sindhiani workers. So, quite scared, I got up and gave everyone water. Not a single woman refused it, and then everyone started clapping. They said we should celebrate with sweets, which we all ate right there! Then we started our meeting.

Once in Kandkot, at a meeting, a woman who was probably a widow, picked up the glass that was on the pitcher and drank water from it. A Hindu woman took offence, said that the woman was from a low caste and got up to leave. The meeting would have broken up in confusion, but I went and stood at the corner of the street. There were some Hindu men standing there too. They were saying that Sindhiani is insulting our religion by forcing us to eat and drink with people of low caste. The Muslim women reacted by saying that as Muslims they could all eat from the same plate and drink from the same glass. Everyone was about to walk out, but I stood on the street and said that there was no great problem. Whoever wished could bring her own glass. It was not necessary to drink from the same one. Then things cooled down.

When there is violence in Sindh, like recently when we burnt their temples, isn't there

tension in Sindhiani as a result?

There was a lot of tension in Kandkot when Muslims burnt their temples.

Was this organised or spontaneous?

It was spontaneous. They heard about the tension over the mosque in India and they burnt the temple in Kandkot. And the women, they said look what the Muslims are doing to us, they've burnt our temples, beat up our people. If we go into your homes, you call us kafir.

We had our meeting three days after the event. So this Muslim woman said: let's hold the meeting in my house, the Hindus are very welcome. The Hindus refused, saying they would not go to any Muslim home and the meeting should be at their place.

These were all Sindhiani women. But communalism had entered our organisation. We met at Lal Chand's house where we had invited both Hindus and Muslims, but Muslims refused to come to a Hindu house. Then I asked one of the girls to spread the mats out in the lane. We placed pitchers of water, got the place ready and finally the women came—Hindus and Muslims from the entire area. We said all this tension because of our different religions is shameful. We are all human beings; others may propagate these differences, but as women we must unite. We are the ones who suffer. We must try to convince our men as well that they are in the wrong. Who says women can't be influential? Let them know how you feel. The meeting went very well, it was open to everyone. We said we did not want the destruction of either mosques or temples. Men came as well, and one of them stood up, obviously in an aggressive mood. I started talking, because I knew a less experienced woman would not be able to handle it. I said: let them come, who are they going to disgrace? We are united and don't care what religion we are. Our religion is our womanhood.

And the men listened?

Yes, they kept standing there and listening.

So there is not much religious tension now in your organisation?

There is no religious tension because there is full religious freedom in Sindhiani.

Class tension?

Yes, in the beginning when we met the landowning women we knew that they were hollow inside, helpless and desperate. But on the outside they were loaded with jewellery and clad in silks and satins. They sat on large beds while slaves and peasant women washed their dishes, swept their houses and served them. They had become used to being waited upon and saw nothing wrong in this.

When we met this one women we said there must be many things in your mind of which you do not speak. If we come to your house your men will not like it. You are proud of being the wife of a wadera, but in fact you have nothing. Can you move with us around town, like your husband does in his jeep whenever he wants, without a veil? Can you vent your anger on your husband, like he can, freely and openly? She said no, she couldn't. So gradually, as we continued to meet, we expressed all the reservations we had and we saw that she was indeed to be pitied. Her status was only for the public. Actually she was like a prisoner in her house. Her mind had become paralysed and she was more to be pitied than the common woman.

The work that you and other Sindhiani members are doing is full of risks. Have you ever had to face any danger or Opposition from your family or the community, from a wadera, or from the maulvi?

Problems can arise, but we are careful in the way we conduct ourselves. If there is a religious function somewhere we are respectful, we are careful how we speak. For instance, if I were to appear without a dupatta and with my hair cut no Sindhi woman would meet me or sit and talk to me. This is where we have lived and grown up, we have to respect the ways of the people here. I can't do whatever *I* like, I have to also consider what people will like.

Interviewed by Nighat Said Khan and Ritu Menon

Illustration courtesy: *Aurat Newsletter*, Lahore

मान, तलाक बिलने किया औरतों का अपमान.
...धर्म मंच.

The personal and the political

an interview-discussion with Shehnaaz Sheikh*

Ritu Menon

Aawaaz-e-Niswaan (Voice of Women) is one of the few organisations of (primarily) Muslim women in India. Started in 1987 by Shehnaaz Sheikh and other Muslim women, it had its meeting place in a tiny, shuttered room in the lower middle class surti mohalla of Nagpada, Bombay. It was loaned to the organisation by Abdul Karim, a sympathiser, and was actually a room in someone's house where members met once a week to discuss their problems — personal, community or, on occasion, national.

Aawaaz-e-Niswaan has a membership of approximately 300-400 women with a core group of about eight, who are active on a regular basis.[1] Only women can register as members but associate membership by men is welcomed and encouraged. From its beginnings in Nagpada it now has branches in other south Bombay localities — Bhendi Bazaar, Umar Khadi and Kamatipura — comprising, as Shehnaaz noted, two parliamentary constituencies.

When she started the organisation, Shehnaaz herself lived on the mezzanine floor of a set of rooms in a typical Bombay chawl. It was a conscious choice, working as she was with women from within the community, organising them to resist their subordinate status and claim their rights. Speaking about the experience of setting up an organisation like Aawaaz-e-Niswaan and reflecting on her own evolution in the process, Shehnaaz touched upon many of the issues that surround the question of identity politics and gender in India today.

"In this community, ours is the only organisation, the only movement, even though it's a women's organisation. We have very few Hindu women, yet it is open to them. In the beginning, some of the Muslim women were very communal — the Hindus have their own organisations, they said — we should follow Islam and all. You know, they are surrounded by maulvis, plus the atmosphere in their homes . . . they do identify with it because they see it every day. There are other problems, too — smugglers, anti-social elements, for

* This discussion and interview took place in 1990, over a period of three days. It would not have been possible without the help and participation of Nandita Gandhi (of the Forum Against the Oppression of Women, Bombay) who clarified many of the issues in subsequent conversations with Shehnaaz in 1991.

instance. Many women wear the burqa because they know that if they wear it, they won't be harassed.

"We want other women in the organisation but we also need some autonomy to begin with. Do you know what happened in Kamatipura? Oh, it was horrible. Kamatipura is half-Hindu, half-Muslim and we had this women's centre in this building in the corner. During a particularly bad riot I discovered that one of our members was storing acid bombs in her house, to be used against the Hindus while fighting was going on. When I objected, the women said, `Yes, ours is a women's organisation, but when there is a riot and violence, we will also close the office and fight in the streets.' `Who will you attack?' I asked them. We discussed it and I said, `Okay, let's fight the Shiv Sena and the police — they are the ones we'll attack.' They said, `No, if their women attack us, we'll fight back.' I said, `But's that's why we have to be together right from the start, so that we don't stone each other'. They didn't agree because they said, `It's our men who will save us not they or theirs'. So I said, `Then let's start with those who are already here. Let's burn these Hindu women.' Then they said, `No, no, they're one of us, they're feminists!'

"So you see, it's a defensive communalism because they're a minority. Another thing: after a few months of working in Kamatipura we wanted to come out with a leaflet and distribute it — in English, Hindi, Urdu and Marathi also — to say we've started a centre for women so that whoever wanted to

come, could. The idea was one, to give publicity, and then to reach out to more women, because from the beginning we've wanted to reach out to both communities and counter the communal situation in this area. Otherwise, it would be taken over by communal forces and become a communal organisation. But at the same time, one had to establish some sort of base in the community if one wanted to change it. So there were these contradictions."

Shehnaaz's own life and her passage from a rebellious college student to a community organiser working against tremendous odds, reflects some of the contradictions she talks about; but it also illustrates the dilemmas and predicaments thrown up by an issue that has come to occupy centre stage for the women's movement in the last ten years, the issue of the increasing communalisation of civil society and political culture, of identity politics, and their intersection with community and gender.

In December 1983 Shehnaaz, then 23 years old, filed a petition in the Supreme Court of India challenging the discrimination against women inherent in Muslim personal law, on issues of polygamy, divorce, maintenance, custody of children and inheritance. Two years earlier, in October 1981, she had been married to a man much older than herself, already married with children. He divorced her unilaterally in 1983 by a triple talaq — the grounds he gave for the divorce were that he found her disobedient and stubborn.

Her petition came up for a hearing in January 1984, was admitted and a notice was sent to the government. Shehnaaz acquired instant fame and was immediately targetted by Muslim fundamentalists for what they saw as her anti-Islam stance. She was opposed by the Muslim Personal Law Board (Bombay), by the Jamaatul Ulema-e-Hind and the Jamaat e Islami, all of which filed different petitions in court challenging the Supreme Court's admission of her plea. Posters denouncing her as a kafir who was endangering Islam were pasted on city walls, death threats were issued against her and she was forced to go into hiding. "If we had met you at that time", she was told later, "we would have shot you."

Not long after Shehnaaz's action, the country found itself polarised along communal lines over the Shah Bano controversy. In April 1985, a Supreme Court judgement granting maintenance from her husband to an indigent, aged Muslim woman under Section 125 of the Criminal Procedure Code, created a furore that reverberated across the country. The Supreme Court verdict ruled that its order to Ahmad Khan, Shah Bano's ex-husband, was not violative of the Shariat (under which Khan had claimed protection, as a Muslim) because it was in keeping with the spirit of the Koran which enjoined all men to look after their wives. Moreover, Shah Bano had sought protection under a section of the CrPc that was intended to curb destitution.

The All India Muslim Personal Law Board and the Shahi Imam of Jama Masjid (Delhi) declared that the Shariat could not be interpreted by anyone other than the ulema, and that the Supreme Court judgement violated the constitutional guarantee of freedom of religious practice. Processions were taken out in Patna and Calicut, petitions signed and protests organised as sections of the Muslim community articulated their response to the judgement, both for and against.

Following the Supreme Court judgement, Shah Bano came under tremendous pressure to retract her claim, to ask for a revocation of the judgement, and affirm the supremacy of Shariat. This she did, eventually, saying, "Most of us read the Koran but do not understand it. I was ignorant when I fought the case all these years. The maulvis have now told us that it would be un-Islamic if I accepted the judgement."[2]

Within the ruling party, one Muslim minister was strongly critical of the ruling, another vocally supportive of it. In the meantime, an independent member of parliament announced his intention of introducing a private member's bill whose provisions would exclude Muslim women from the purview of Section 125 of the CrPC.

Communal and fundamentalist organisations, democratic rights and civil liberties groups, political parties and women's organisations, all made representations to the ruling Congress (I) government, highlighting different aspects of the issue. Yet, as different analyses of the Shah Bano controversy have shown,[3] the one thing they all managed to do was to subordinate the gender question to all others — minority and identity politics, vote bank calculations, party politics, State collusion with fundamentalist forces, and so on. Except for the women's movement which, through protests, demonstrations, signature and leaflet campaigns, and finally legal action (17 women's organisations challenged the constitutional validity of the Muslim Women's (Protection of Rights on Divorce) Bill when it was passed in May 1986) sought to keep the issue of women's equality before the law and in the Constitution, paramount. Even so, so ambivalent were the positions on women, religion and community identity that within the movement old differences and debates on the desirability of a uniform civil code for all communities surfaced again and temporarily shifted the focus away from Shah Bano.

Shehnaaz herself, who at the time was actively associated with two women's organisations in Bombay (Forum Against the Oppression of Women and Women's Centre) disagreed strongly with both groups on renewing the demand for a uniform civil code, although the issue of personal laws had always been on the agenda cf both organisations. At the time, she says she believed, along with reformers like Asghar Ali Engineer and others, that such a demand must come from within the Muslim community.

"We debated the UCC a lot but even in the women's movement I felt my minority status, felt this is Hindu feminism. They are all very nice people, but they're not trying to understand me. I have something to say . . . when I say they were Hindu feminists, I mean it more culturally because I identify with them also, very much. But, for example, when the question of Muslim women came up, say Shah Bano, then how many Muslim women did you ask what they wanted? At that time, there was no Aawaaz-e-Niswaan, and I was in a minority amongst them."

Did she feel, then, that consensus was necessary for any progressive action?

"Somewhere, yes. Now, these are Muslim women; they are women, yes, but they're also Muslims, a minority within a minority. Their minority status determines the difference. Their first identity is as that, more than as women . . .

"In the Shah Bano case, it was a straightforward case of maintenance. People just brought up the UCC — there was no need to bring it up. You talk of coming into the mainstream — there are no Muslim women in workers' or women's movements. Now that I'm working in the community, I realise it. In order to enter the mainstream you have to create some kind of a stream first, otherwise you're imposing something as an outsider — if they don't accept it, then what's the use?

"You see, the whole thing (Shah Bano, the UCC) was taken up by the Hindu fundamentalists and they kept attacking the Muslims. When this happens the women are in a real fix because they want their identity, and their fight is more difficult because they have to fight the fundamentalists in their own community and also the fundamentalists from the outside . . . it's not that all women demand a change, but the movement must come from within the community that raises it. Women's opposition is there, definitely, and they have to fight it themselves, they have to organise, but as a minority they are beleaguered — and there also the women suffer.

"On the UCC, actually, we should frame it differently, call it a women's code, and that's what we've been calling for from Aawaaz-e-Niswaan from day one. That's how we avoid the religious framework — we say we need one law for all women and the women agree. It should be equal rights for women and everyone should participate."

A combination of factors (including, perhaps, an unarticulated realisation that the emphasis by the women's movement on a woman's gender identity obscured other identities, as strong) led Shehnaaz to temporarily hold back on

her own petition that was pending in the Supreme Court. This was both strategically desirable as well as politically necessary for her at the time. The fall-out from the Shah Bano controversy once again highlighted her own physical vulnerability, and "because of this I thought I should bring it up at the right time, with the support of Muslim women. It's not just a legal battle — you can win it in the courts but lose outside, like Shah Bano."

In her own life and in her family, says Shehnaaz, there has always been a history of struggle. Her grandmother migrated to Bombay from Lahore after Partition, in itself a curious event for it was not usual for a Muslim family in Lahore to have opted for India at the time. Moreover, she had separated from her husband sometime before that ("He was no use," she used to tell Shehnaaz, "a good-for-nothing, all he could do was romance") and arrived in Bombay with her daughter and son, Shehnaaz's father, who was then in his late teens. She lived in a slum colony (kachhi basti) and reared sheep and goats for a living.

"It was a hard life, but my grandmother was a fighter. Where they lived there were a lot of pathans, and she had a certain sense of style, dressed differently and all. And she was alone. She had a thirteen year old daughter and my mother, who was only 15 when she married my father. Now, my grandmother was strong, but sometimes I feel that women like her internalise patriarchal values and attitudes. She could fight, she became like a man, she became protective towards my mother. And they were poor. They had only one pair of slippers, so if one of them went out the others had to stay in. And then, they were feudal too — can't send young girls out to work and all that . . ."

Her upbringing, Shehnaaz says, was only conventionally religious in the beginning, the religiosity just symbolic, ". . . pray, fast and all, which I see in Nagpada even now, it's like any other collective activity. When we were children, religious instruction was like other instruction — be good, do well, behave — and I didn't feel oppressed by it. In fact, I was quite religious myself, kept all the fasts, read the namaaz and all. We used to go to a madrassa once a week and I would read the namaaz five times a day till I was about 13 or 14. If I missed it in school, I would come home and make up for it on my own."

Then, in 1971, during the Bhiwandi riots, her father's garage was burnt down and he was rendered jobless. He spent most of his time at home reading the Koran, graduallly becoming what Shehnaaz calls a "revisionist", not allowing her mother even to wear a sari. Her grandmother, too, who earlier wouldn't even read the namaaz, became quite "orthodox" after all the "danga-phasad" (rioting). Shehnaaz attributes some of her father's and grandmother's "fundamentalism" to their self-perception as belonging to a beleaguered community, post-Partition. "Partition *ke baad,*identity crisis to *zaroor hua hai,logon ko bahut mahsus hota hai, yeh sab.* This feeling of being a minority, at that time I couldn't understand it. On the one hand they were educating me in a convent, on the other, such strict religiosity at home." Not very long after this, Shehnaaz began to feel constricted by the contradictory messages she was getting from the instruction she received at school and instructions at home. Her favourite subject, she says, was history, "and they kept telling us about secularism, secularism, secularism. And my best friends were Hindus or Christians. But at home they were always saying `*Sale Hindu, kafir, maar dala mussalmanon ko'.* (Damn Hindus, infidels, they've killed the Muslims.) They teach you one thing and do something else. So when I approached Mt. Mary I would make the sign of the cross and be roundly abused at home. So there was all this strong Christian, strong Islamic, strong secular business. I just couldn't understand. But I couldn't also challenge it in any way because the home atmosphere was so oppressive. They told me you only study there, you're not supposed to make friends with them."

Shehnaaz did challenge all this however, not only at home, but in the Supreme Court when she questioned the constitutional validity of Muslim personal law in 1983. While at home, she began arguing with her father as he became more and more orthodox, saying she wouldn't pray till she could see "this God". Her mother's religiosity, she believes, was real rather than symbolic and enabled her to cope with her life. In a sense, her father's was real too — he didn't drink, for instance. But he could get, and often was, violent. *"Islam mein gussa haram hai,"* Shehnaaz would remind him and get soundly beaten for her impertinence.

"At Aawaaz-e-Niswaan, the Koran has symbolic value, just reciting, nothing more. We have said, keep religion at home, because if we get into it there'll be a lot of problems. But if one is working with people one has to acknowledge it because you can't hurt their sentiments. It is very dear to them, they believe in it, and you can conscientize without hurting them. I never comment on religion — if I did, many would simply leave without even a dialogue. So, we just say it's a personal matter, keep religion at home."

Yet, in Aawaaz-e-Niswaan's experience, a large number of the cases it deals with are those of unilateral divorce or maintenance, both governed by Muslim personal law which, in turn, is a matter of extreme religious and cultural significance, contentious debate and political volatility. With Islam, an avowedly public and congregational religion with carefully regulated codes of social and moral conduct — and one, moreover, that from the very beginning, was constituted as a state — the desire to keep religion at home is often thwarted. At times, it is simply impossible. In Shehnaaz's own case, her challenging Muslim personal law on constitutional grounds apparently held no religious significance for her and need not have been construed as any irreverence towards Islam on her part. Just as, obstensibly, Shah Bano's was a straightforward maintenance issue, so Shehnaaz's petition pleaded gender bias; in making their action *legal and public*, however, they provoked the rallying cry of "Islam in danger" which immediately subordinated gender to community and religion and, simultaneously, catapulted both Shehnaaz and Shah Bano into the political domain. Once this displacement had taken place and the issues raised by the two women claimed, variously, by political parties, the women's movement, religious organisations, community leaders and the government, Shehnaaz Sheikh and Shah Bano became symbolic of minority identity: their individual, gender identities were eclipsed even as they became the subjects of contending discourses — political, legal, feminist and religious.

Were they to be protected? Denounced? Upheld? If protected, then by whom? Their religion, community and families, or their government, their country and their Constitution? How was their denunciation to be understood and countered? How could their rights as women be secured or safeguarded? Which of their multiple identities — gender, class, community or religious — was to be asserted and validated or redefined and reinforced? And where were these boundaries of identity to be drawn?

That women themselves partially embody and define community identity, and that this identity is continually constructed and reconstructed in response to social, political and economic pressures, makes the question of allowing religion to remain a personal matter, problematic. As a consequence of the fall-out of their individual actions, *as Muslim women*, both Shah Bano and Shehnaaz Sheikh were forced into altering their course of action: Shah Bano, under pain of proving her credentials as a good Muslim, retracted her plea for maintenance under Section 125 of the CrPC, declaring that the Shariat was greater than any other form of law and asking for the judgement to be revoked. The reasons she gave for her action were local, social ostracism, pressure of public opinion and persuasion by the maulvis. Shehnaaz Sheikh, in the face of death threats by Muslim fundamentalist organisations, who accused her of being a kafir and of having joined hands with the Rashtriya Swayam sevak Sangh , first went into hiding and then sought the support of women's groups. After the passage of the Muslim Women's Bill she joined the Lawyers' Collective in Bombay in June 1986 and embarked on a survey of Muslim women seeking protection under Section 125 of the CrPC.

Both Shah Bano and Shehnaaz Sheikh had, in other words, transgressed the boundaries of community identity by asserting their gender identity and claiming their rights *as women*, equal in the eyes of the law, whose equality, moreover, was a fundamental right guaranteed by a secular Constitution. By placing themselves outside the purview of Muslim personal law they were undermining both its sanctity and authority, thus galvanising sections of the Muslim community into once again defining itself in relation to the majority community by reasserting its "Islamic" character. It was this character that the women were seen to be violating by not conforming. Their infidelity to the institution of marriage as prescribed, to their community and, ultimately, to their religion was compounded by their making public what was, properly speaking, a personal matter.

When she challenged the validity of Muslim personal law in the Supreme Court, Shehnaaz says it was her identity as a woman that she was most acutely aware of: ". . . the Muslim bit came later, before that it was a personal battle. Then I came into contact with the women's movement and I became conscious of that factor. Now, I'm more aware of the community, I can analyse it more objectively, understand it and find solutions, and I can understand exactly what individual women go through.

"At Aawaaz-e-Niswaan, our experience has been similar. Women under-stand their own oppression in spite of their religious beliefs. They know that their laws do not give them the justice they want. On the other hand the men uphold Islamic laws, *uspe zor denge*, just to protect themselves. But that does not mean that the women do not believe in Allah Mian.

"Class makes a big difference. Working class men and women have very little time for all this because they are busy trying to survive. One can reach out to them easily. They understand that if religion is brought out on the streets there will be bloodshed because they suffer the most. In Aawaaz . . . I have noticed that women react differently to this, some stay and others leave. Women believe in religion and you cannot take away this belief without giving them an alternative. Some, because they suffer, are willing to look beyond religion — they fight and come back. Others leave. Perhaps we have not been able to give them an alternative, but we can't just lose them, we have to do something."

The question of where the boundaries of identity are to be drawn is a recurring one. In Aawaaz-e-Niswaan it has manifested itself variously in different circumstances. Should community identity take precedence over gender when it comes to membership? When instances of communal violence take place and women retreat into what Shehnaaz calls "defensive communalism" does that imply that they are necessarily more community-oriented than oriented against violence and for women? In challenging biases and discrimina-

Karen Haydock

tion on the grounds of personal law, should women have to choose between their faith and their rights? And in their symbolic role as markers of community identity, should they be required to endorse fundamentalist practice in order to uphold religiosity? How does their status as a minority within a minority, and as members of a particular class, intersect with the larger communities of which they are a part?

These sometimes harmonious, often colliding and generally overlapping identities are something Shehnaaz herself has been aware of since early childhood, through the figures of her grandmother and parents. An early apprehension of difference came when she learnt that her mother was a Christian. She ran away from home to marry her father when she was still a minor, only 15 years old. Her parents opposed the match vigorously, but she wanted to be a good wife, and therefore also a good Muslim. "My mother's conflict was not so much a conflic between her Christianity and Islam, but of values — keeping herself covered, for example." Although the marriage had its share of problems she would always side with her husband when it came to major decisions. According to Shehnaaz, "She could never take a stand and so she couldn't stop my marriage."

When Shehnaaz was 19 years old, she was despatched to Jaipur where her aunt and grandmother had found a match for her — a Ph.D. who was quite progressive, whose sister had married outside the community and who had made his mother cast off the veil when she was quite old. But Shehnaaz wanted to study, not get married. Still, after meeting and talking to the young man, she found she liked him and he told her she could continue to study after they were married. It was all arranged but, in an ironic reversal, the marriage had to be called off because the Jamaat found him unacceptable for some reason. She returned to Bombay where she spent the time as though she were in jail, cooking and cleaning. "I hated it. That was the first time I started feeling the burden of being a woman. *Yeh kya hai?* First they cut your wings and then they say you can't fly. I was just stagnating, waiting to get married, to get out. I couldn't bear it. Then this guy came along who had no problem with my leg (*ek badi thi, ek choti*) and in 15 days we had got married! He was double my age, married already. I didn't know he had a wife and children in the village."

Shehnaaz's experience of marriage was, if anything, even more oppressive than her life at home. Her husband was unkind, fault-finding and sexually perverted. Apart from periodic violent outbursts of temper, he had virtually no communication with her. "I don't know, *mujhe chun chun ke* samples *mile hain!* I used to think there must be something wrong with me." She began resisting him not only physically, but generally. He responded by locking her in, stopped her allowance, brought his son to live with them, and finally just threw her out, saying she was too obdurate for her own good.

After this she was virtually without succour, dependent on people's charity. She sought refuge in a neighbour's house, but had to leave in haste when he tried to misbehave with her. She slept where she could, including railway waiting-rooms and offices (where she was locked in one night by her boss, and slept on the office desk). She worked in a private firm for Rs.500 a month, but couldn't find anywhere to stay as hostels had no place for her. Finally she found two old women who lived within walking distance of her office, who took her in. The two were very kind to her and for the first time in a long while she was at peace with herself.

She continued to be harassed in one way or another, however, by her husband's relatives, and realised that she would have to be free of him once and for all. She consulted various people, including some kazis, who informed her that she could exercise her right to khula (divorce) but would have to forfeit her meher(dower). That was when she says she was filled with anger at being left with nothing but suffering as a result of her marriage. She consulted a lawyer who was knowledgeable about Muslim personal law and filed her petition in the Supreme Court.

Would she characterise her relationship with religion, too, as one of continuous struggle?

"No, only struggle wouldn't be correct. In college I took philosophy, so this whole religion thing came up. Those who believe in god offer you only indirect proof, but I believe in reality. *Jo* indirect *hai, uski to baat hi nahin banti.* I've always been like that. If there's no proof, it doesn't exist. But sometimes it seems like there is some supernatural power — I have also been in that state — but that is spirituality. Religion *mein* dependence *hai,* spirituality *mein ziada* freedom *hai,* liberation *hai.*

"And then, religion has always been synonymous with male chauvinism for me. My father used to say to me, `You're a woman, *yeh karna hai, woh nahin karna* — do this, don't do that, don't stare at me, don't raise your voice. How dare you? Islam *mein kaha hai . . .'* But he also did many un-Islamic things, he used to get violent, so my resentment began with that. I prayed and fasted and all that, but I resented this.

"In my father's home I really had to fight because religion was used to suppress us, to shut us up. Then later in marriage it came up, but there were other problems. Then I was alone — during the early stages of the struggle it was very difficult, very taxing, and I felt very alone. For three months I was running from place to place. Then those two women with whom I stayed, they really used to pray! *Puja bhi karte the, Koran bhi* — they were Hindus, but married to Muslims. With them I started praying again. They didn't force me or anything, I just prayed as a kind of meditation. I started reciting the Koran because it gave me peace. If I had had an okay marriage maybe I wouldn't have rebelled in this way. Sometimes when the oppression is very, very direct, then these things happen.

"When I started reading the Koran for my petition I became interested in some of the progressive things it was saying for women. I liked those, but then in the same Koran there were other things that were very oppressive, so I never really believed in it — there was never a question about there being a god or anything. But you know, now I think about it, because one didn't have a definite ideology, my mind was going round and round. The world around you is religious, there are norms, it's there everywhere. At that time I didn't know any marxists or feminists, I didn't even know there were people who didn't believe and weren't religious. And in society you have to conform to something.

"Now the thing about bringing out the good points of religion, any religion, means that there is a danger of glorifying it and that may lead to greater

Karen Haydock

communalism. Most people's belief is symbolic, customary, but it can be oppressive. And then, it's misused by all those who want to— even gang-wars, Muslim or Hindu, are just masked by all this religious business. Basically, they're just goondas. When we took this up in Aawaaz-e-Niswaan, the women said, yes, religious processions should be banned, there's so much eve-teasing, so much violence."

Nevertheless, when they were caught in the middle of a riot the question came up again and again with renewed urgency. "Once, when a riot had taken place between Bohras and Sunnis in Kamatipura, we wanted to meet and discuss it, make a statement condemning it, but the woman in whose house we used to meet said, No. They were really communal — they said, Their men come and instigate violence here and abuse our women (this was the Bohri women); finally everybody said, *Nahin, galat baat hai*; but that was only because we had been talking about women's oppression and how, in riots, women are the worst victims, always.

"When it came to taking in non-Muslim members, however, they said, why should we help them? During a riot, it's their men who beat us with stones and our men who protect us. And they have enough organisations, anyway. This kind of thing always came up. I told you we had these two non-Muslim members, so I said, okay, let's burn them first. Then they thought about it and said, '*Nahin, yeh sab auraton ka sawal hai*' (No, this is a question that concerns all women.)"

The woman question itself, however, can be posed in a variety of ways, to reflect a predominant concern or identity at a particular moment in time — it can be articulated as one of gender, of class, caste, community or religion, of race or even of nationality, and each of these is a constituent factor in what is termed identity politics. Each of these, moreover, may be asserted independently of, or in correspondence with, one or more of the others over a period of time, to make up a whole that defies a single, unitary — or even consistent — definition. The assertion of one over the other(s) is generally determined by one's location within a particular group as it intersects and interacts with other groups in society, through social, political and economic processes that are in dynamic relation with each other.

Thus, Shehnaaz's personal biography is mediated by her political history, which in turn has been influenced by the struggles she has had to undertake and the choices she has made — as a woman, a Muslim, a middle class activist working in a poor Muslim community, a lawyer and, finally, a Marxist feminist.

In 1991, Aawaaz-e-Niswaan formally affiliated itself with the National Federation of Indian Women, the women's wing of the Communist Party of India.

This has entailed a structural change in the organisation which was formerly made up of a loosely-held group of women, and characterised by a flexibility of form and choice of strategy. Now, according to Shehnaaz, it is more "bureau-cratic" and disciplined, has more rules and regulations (members have to register themselves, for example) and is less informal. This, she feels, will help consolidate its membership and reduce the chances of its being "used" by other (clearly undesirable) groups or forces. It is a significant shift for the organisation, especially as it has resisted any association with political parties in the past. Speaking about formalising its activities, Shehnaaz dwelt on the history and experiences of the organisation that led them into taking such a step.

"When I started, in my mind the idea was that Muslim women have to fight for their rights and for that we have to get organised. But what kind of an organisation, even I didn't know. I wasn't sure that even five women would come together — there's this whole history, it would keep breaking for so many years, all these middle class women and intellectuals, and finally I went to Nagpada where I found all these women. Even over here it was somewhat like the Forum (Forum Against the Oppression of Women), very loose, and I liked that — there's more equality, you can say what you like — but for bringing social reform to a community, it can't remain like this. That's too big a task.

"For me, it was trial and error. I'd never been in a political party and there was no one to guide me. I didn't want to function like a party, because after all it's a women's organisation. But slowly, the membership increased and it became more of a mass organisation. . . So then the whole question of an ideology came up because we had to be clear on all this, it can't just be abstract. Feminism is like that sometimes. Then, it was not a middle class organisation — there was nobody earning, not even me, so it was quite difficult. One had to give it some kind of form because we did manage to initiate some sort of a social reform movement, with women not only participating but in the leadership.

"Now, basically, I'm a Marxist, but I'm also a feminist, so in Aawaaz-e-Niswaan I was very clear that patriarchy and women would not play second fiddle to class struggle. (You can see how even socialist countries have adapted to patriarchy!) Because I had these differences I didn't join any party: first, there was the question of women, and then there was the minority question. This is a minority community and I didn't want it to be annexed by the mainstream. It had to be autonomous and have women in the leadership. I think I can say that we have been successful in this, five per cent, because women *have* taken the leadership — even men with problems come to us because there's no other movement. It's a new experiment and I think it was needed here, because the kind of oppression there is in this community was surprising even to me.

Women are really treated like *kachra* here — when we used to go from house to house earlier, people used to ask *kya tumhare gharon mein mard nahin hai*, why have you come? So for women to take to the streets in a morcha is a revolution in the Muslim community, because they never used to come out even during festivals.

"Now, I had learnt a lot of things from my association with Marxist-feminist women's groups and their analysis of society, but the first thing that struck me was: they say they're a women's group but they can't even relate to a woman — we don't do case work, they say! First of all we don't see women as "cases", but what it means is that even though on paper you say you're working against patriarchy, your focus is still on class struggle. To me, as a women's organisation, your focus can't be on class struggle — that your union or your party does — your focus *has* to be on women. There are certain issues like women's oppression within the family which you just can't ignore because the class organisation will break!

"Then, the whole question of identifying with women, sharing, that just wasn't there. And ideologically, they didn't have anything for Muslims, for the minorities, and they don't really have anything to deal with patriarchy. Don't anger the men, they say, you have to work with the masses. So masses is men — full stop!

"Then they say, we don't glorify personal struggle — nobody's saying glorify it, we all know that collectives give more strength — but then I used to feel *my* struggle is useless, it has no value. I'm not saying you have to glorify but somewhere you need to talk about it, because it's only when we give space to women that they develop. For instance, I think the most difficult thing is for a single woman to struggle alone — now, if you say *that's* no struggle, look at the dalits, look at the oppressed, *they're* struggling, then a woman can feel, well, I have no place here. If my struggle is a closed space, then you're denying my strength. Maybe they get their strength from listening to someone or being inspired by a book or whatever, but I got mine from my struggle."

Interviewed by Ritu Menon and Kamla Bhasin

Notes

1 These figures are as of 1990, and may have changed since.
2 Reported in the *Times of India*, January 2, 1986.
3 Zoya Hasan, "Minority Identity, Muslim Women's Bill Campaign and the Political Process", *Economic and Political Weekly*, January 7, 1989; Zakia Pathak and Rajeshwari Sunder Rajan, "Shah Bano", *Signs*, vol. 14, no. 3, 1989; Rohini Hensman, "Oppression Within Oppression:: The Dilemma of Muslim Women in India", Working Paper 1, Women Living Under Personal Laws Network, Combaillaux, 1989; Shahida Lateef, *Muslim Women in India: Political and Private Realities* (Delhi: Kali for Women, 1990).

Notes on contributors

Amrita Chhachhi is Lecturer in Women's Studies at the Institute of Social Studies, The Hague. She has published numerous articles on women and industrialisation and on the State and fundamentalism in S. Asia. She is co-editor of a book, *Confronting the State, Capital and Patriarchy: Women Organising in the Process of Industrialisation* (forthcoming).

Shahnaz Rouse is Professor of Sociology at Sarah Lawrence College, New York. She has written and published widely on women, the State and fundamentalism in Islamic societies.

Gabriele Dietrich teaches in the Department of Social Analysis at the Tamil Theological Seminary, Madurai. She has been involved with the workers', women's, and alternative health movements in India for many years, and written extensively on all. She is the author of *Women's Movement in India: Conceptual and Religious Reflections*, and *Culture, Religion and Development*.

Indira Jaising is an eminent civil rights lawyer who has been in the forefront of pressing for gender-sensitive laws in India. She is editor of *the Lawyers* and has written widely on women and law.

Shahla Zia is a lawyer by profession, and full-time member of the Aurat Foundation, Islamabad.

Rubina Saigol is an active member of the Women's Action Forum, and works with Applied Socio-Economic Research (ASR), Lahore.

Anita Rampal is a member of Ekalavya, an ngo working on non-formal science education in Madhya Pradesh, India. A scientist and educationist, she is currently a Fellow at Nehru Memorial Museum & Library, New Delhi.

Mirai Chatterjee has been a full-time member of the Self-Employed Women's Association (SEWA), Ahmedabad, for many years.

Mary Roy is Principal of Corpus Christi High School in Kerala, India.

Shiraz Sidhva is a correspondent with *The Financial Times* (India), and has covered Kashmir on a sustained basis for the last five years.

Paola Bacchetta is presently a doctoral candidate in Sociology at Institute d'etudes du Developpement Economique et Social (IEDES), Universite de Paris I, Pantheon-Sorbonne. She has published widely in France and the USA on racism and sexism, and on French feminism.

Ritu Menon is co-founder of Kali for Women, (Delhi). She has written widely on women and media, women and violence and women and fundamentalism, and is working, with Kamla Bhasin, on an oral history of women's experiences of the Partition of India.

Kamla Bhasin has been active in the area of women and development for the last twenty years. She has written extensively on participatory training in development; on women; on sustainable development; and is the author of numerous activist songs and non-sexist books for children.

Nighat Said Khan is Director of Applied Socio-Economic Research (ASR), Lahore. Active in the left and women's movements in Pakistan, she is a founder-member of Women's Action Forum (WAF), Lahore. Social activist, video film-maker and writer, she is the author of several pamphlets and reports on women and development in Pakistan, and editor of *Voices Within: Dialogues with Women on Islam.*

KALI FOR WOMEN

Kali for Women, India's first women's publishing house, is concerned primarily with publishing Third World studies on women. Set up as a Trust, its objective is to increase the body of knowledge on women in the Third World, to give voice to such knowledge as already exists, and to provide a forum for women writers, creative and academic. It has initiated various programmes aimed at producing reasonably priced published material in the social sciences and humanities, general non-fiction, fiction, including pamphlets and monographs. Its books are published all over the world in several languages, reaching a wide range of readers.

In addition, Kali collaborates regularly with other women's organisations and networks nationally, regionally and internationally, on a range of issues and projects on women. It is active in the women's movement in India, participating in campaigns, conferences and consultations on issues taken up by the movement, from time to time. It has also been a part of the ongoing discussions on women's studies in India, and co-ordinated several thematic discussions for the Indian Association of Women's Studies on women, media and culture. On request, we provide editorial and production services to other women's organisations, within India and outside.

Regionally and internationally, Kali is part of the continuing activity around women and alternative communication, and the dissemination of women and development material.

Kali for Women
B 1/8 Hauz Khas
New Delhi 110 016
Tel: 685 2530; 686 4497
Fax: 91-11-686 6720

ISIS INTERNATIONAL

Isis International is an international non-governmental women's organization, founded in 1974 to promote the empowerment of women through information sharing, communication and networking. Its network reaches over 50,000 individuals and organizations in 150 countries, from grassroots groups to policy makers. Isis International's activities include resource centres and information sharing, publications and communications, health networking, advocacy of women's issues and skills sharing. It has two offices: one in Santiago, Chile and the other in Manila, Philippines.

Isis International Resource Centres

The Resource Centre of each office houses a collection of documentation and information from all over the world on a wide range of development and women's issues. This information is processed by the Resource Centre and Information Programme of each office and incorporated into bibliographic, human resources and databases. It is made available to all interested groups, institutions and individuals through information services and specialized publications including resource directories, bibliographic catalogues and publications on specific themes. The Resource Centres are also open to visitors.

Regular Resource Centre publications include the bilingual *Base de Datos Mujer - Women's Data Base* and *Documentas,* a bibliographic bulletin in Spanish, from our office in Chile and *Resource Update,* a bibliographic bulletin and Information Packs on key issues, in English from our office in the Philippines.

Isis International Publications

The Communication Networking Programme of each office publishes a quarterly magazine: *Mujeres en Action,* in Spanish, from our office in Chile and *Women in Action,*in English, from our office in the Philippines. These publications bring together information, analyses and perspectives about and from women around the world and serve as communication channels for sharing ideas, experiences and models of organization and action. Books on key issues are published twice a year in Spanish through the Isis International *Ediciones de las Mujeres* in Chile and on an occasional basis in English through the Isis International Book Series in the Philippines.

The *Women's Health Journal* in English is published by the Health Networking Programme of our office in Chile with the collaboration of the office in the Philippines. The office in Chile also publishes the Spanish language *Revista de la Red Salud de las Mujeres Latino Americanas y del Caribe. Women Envision,* a monthly newsletter in English is published by the Advocacy and Campaigns Programme in our office in the Philippines. It contains information on activities leading up to the World Conference and NGO Forum in China 1995 and other international meetings and campaigns.

Health Networking

The Health Networking Programme of our office in Chile coordinates the Latin American and Caribbean Women's Health Network while the office in the Philippines undertakes health networking activities in the Asia-Pacific Region. Both offices offer health information services and resource materials.

Advocacy, Campaigns and Policy

Our office in Chile coordinates the Information and Policy Programme on Violence Against Women in Latin America and the Caribbean. The Advocacy and Campaigns Programme of the office in the Philippines produces Action Alerts on campaigns, actions and solidarity appeals of women's groups and networks around the world.

Networking Services

Both offices offer referral and assistance to individuals and organizations, locally and internationally, in linking with others around the world.

Training

Both offer technical assistance and training in communication and information management and in the use of new information technologies.

SOUTH ASIAN WOMEN'S FORUM

South Asian Women's Forum (SAWF) is an informal network of women activists, researchers and other women concerned with and working on women's issues. SAWF was set up in 1977 with the objective of building a network of women's organisations and activities in the Asian and Pacific region to enable them to keep in touch with each other, co-operate in developing future programmes, and support each other in searching for solutions to common problems.

SAWF's office is in Colombo, Sri Lanka.